PLANET
PARENT

THE WORLD'S BEST
WAYS TO BRING UP
YOUR CHILDREN

MARK WOODS

Planet Parent: The world's best ways to bring up your children

This first edition published in 2015 by White Ladder Press, an imprint of Crimson Publishing Ltd, 19–21c Charles Street, Bath BA1 1HX.

© Mark Woods 2015

British Library Cataloguing in Publication Data
A catalogue record for this book is available from the British Library.

ISBN 978 1 90828 180 7

Typeset by IDSUK (DataConnection) Ltd

Printed and bound in Malta by Gutenberg Press Ltd

For Sarah, Stan, Louis and Nancy.

Contents

*Away from the slick science, are we too quick to forget
the planet's fertility rites, potions and practices?
We discover what's tosh and what's true.*

*In just 35 years the assisted fertility industry has become a
billion-pound business – are the rules the same the world over?*

*Being pregnant is a special time wherever you are – but who really
looks after their mums the best and how do they do it?*

*From its brutal history to its modern medical manifestation,
where, how and with whom a mother brings a baby into the
world differ wildly from place to place.*

3 Looking after baby

The first year: Global game plans for the biggest job of your life

As learning curves go, there's nothing steeper than the introduction to parenthood. From how we all play the name game to who knows best where baby is concerned, we look at how the planet's parents employ different strategies to ensure their babies survive and thrive.

Sleep: Do parents everywhere feel this knackered?

Swaddling, co-sleeping, on the back, on the front – the way babies sleep has created a myriad of tips, techniques and even the odd tear – but has anyone really cracked it?

Driving the planet potty: Toilet training tips from the East

The world is split down the middle when it comes to teaching children how to become masters of their own number ones and twos. How and why do China and India make the potty redundant so early on?

4 Food

Of bottles and breastfeeds: Who does what on the great milk merry-go-round?

Wet nurses, formula, the bottle wars – how is the fierce debate about breast being best played out around the planet?

One more mouthful: What do the world's children eat?

Does every culture share the same issues when it comes to feeding their young? Does everyone have fish fingers at their disposal? Is the well-heralded French revolution in avoiding a picky young eater and a poorly fed adult the only show in town?

7 The finishing touches 201

About the author

Mark Woods started his writing career as a news journalist before moving into public relations for a television company. The enormous corporate disaster that followed allowed Mark to concentrate on writing and he joined the charity Comic Relief as a journalist and Twitter man.

The birth of his first son inspired Mark to write the bestselling *Pregnancy for Men*, which has since been translated into seven languages. His next parenting instalment, *Babies and Toddlers for Men*, aimed to help the modern day father make the best fist of the very early days of being a dad.

Now *Planet Parent* shares the best tips, secrets and historical wisdom from around the world when it comes to bringing up our children the best we possibly can.

Or at least not making a total hash of it.

Acknowledgements

Enormous thanks to all the contributors to *Planet Parent*; your personal perspectives are easily the most powerful part of the book.

To the entire team at Crimson, especially Hugh Brune and Sam Bacon, much gratitude, not only for the professionalism but also for the patience shown during the lengthy writing process. Many thanks also to Rebecca Winfield, my ever invaluable and insightful agent.

Most of all, love and thanks to my extraordinary wife Sarah, beautiful boys Stan and Louis and the glorious, gorgeous little reason why this book is quite a bit later than originally intended, Nancy Lois Woods.

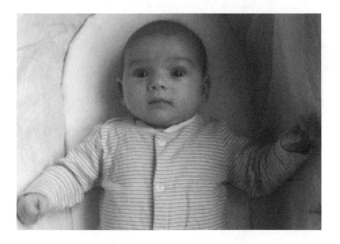

Introduction

Nothing has the ability to hit you where it hurts quite like being a parent.

There's the unbridled joy of course, the moments of golden, glorious wonder when we are privileged to witness something so beautiful, so noble and so perfect that we can scarcely contain ourselves.

But it comes at a cost and that cost is caring. Caring about what happens to your children like you care about nothing else on earth.

This isn't an intellectual decision to care either. It's not something you choose to feel or have the ability to switch off. You can distract yourself from it, pretend you've beaten or becalmed it, but you haven't. It's always there.

Whether it's a pet lip in the baby bath, a shunned hand of friendship in the playground or teenage troubles at home, we are, as parents, all utterly, horribly vulnerable to the challenges thrown up by trying to raise our children.

In a bid to try to avoid these emotional bear traps, the vast majority of parents go to extraordinary lengths to ensure that they do the very best for their offspring at all times.

From sleeping patterns and school places to obesity and overpraising, we seek out advice, check facts and pore over research, in the hope that it will enable us to make the best decisions and choices for our precious charges.

For generations the pool of knowledge from which parents could draw was a fairly localised one. Friends and family were by far our biggest influencers and so the way we raised our children tended to follow a similar pattern to how we had been brought up ourselves.

The world, though, has changed.

Just as what we eat, how we communicate and the entertainment we consume has gone global, so the way the rest of the world brings up their young has begun to enter our consciousness too – albeit in a rather piecemeal and disjointed fashion.

While the core issues may be the same for parents everywhere, how each country and culture tackle them can be astonishingly different, with age-old traditions and new thinking often coming together to produce an illuminating solution or approach.

What this book aims to do is gather together the best and most helpful of these nuggets of international information in one place to create the beginnings of a global support system for us all.

Among many other things, we'll look at the ingenious way in which many Chinese parents tackle potty training, how the French buck the unhealthy eating trends prevalent among much of the world's young, and exactly why Finland and South Korea are consistently found to have the world's best education systems, despite having diametrically opposing approaches.

Much of what we'll learn along the way will be inspiring, some will be surprising, some may even be shocking, but I hope that all the wisdom unearthed here will be helpful in doing the most important job any of us will ever have: raising our children in the best way we possibly can.

Welcome to Planet Parent.

1
Fertility far and wide

Fertility
Hit and myth

I t can be tempting in this day and age to be blinded by the science that surrounds issues like fertility and to marvel at the modernity of the potential solutions being developed by the white coat brigade.

There are more myths, rituals and beliefs from around the world concerning all aspects of how we procreate than you'll find attached to almost anything else we hold dear as a species. It's perhaps understandable that we can scoff somewhat at the basic homespun nature of what people used to believe – or in some cases still do – when we compare it with the super-scientific approach that has been dominant over the past couple of decades.

These beliefs don't all consist of quirky old wives' tales either; occasionally they are incredibly widespread, cast iron, nailed on truths about fertility and birth rates that sweep entire cultures. But even these can occasionally turn to mush on closer inspection.

Take the population explosion, a topic that Swedish statistician superstar (a more unlikely title it's hard to imagine, I'll grant you) Hans Rosling has shown to be one of the most misunderstood across the planet.

The widely held belief is that the increase in the number of our species is inexorable, a rise that can never be checked.

Not so, says Hans.

Half a century ago, the average world fertility rate was five babies born per woman on the planet. Today, despite most of us thinking the opposite, that key number has fallen to 2.5.[1] That's an astonishing shift and one driven by a potent mix of a lower infant mortality rate, access to contraception and, crucially, female education – put 'the girl effect' into a search engine of your choosing to find out why that's such a powerful combination of factors.

This represents a huge global success story and one that goes hand in hand with another often misunderstood fact, namely that most of what's termed the Third World is on a trajectory towards health and prosperity, with many countries doing it at twice the pace that the West managed.[2]

The demographic consequences of the drop in global fertility are profound, with figures showing that the number of children in the world today is the most there will be for a very long time indeed.

That's right – according to many experts, as a species we are about to enter the era of 'peak child'. In all likelihood it'll take the best part of the rest of this century for the slowdown in population growth to turn into a full-blown halt, but that is what is being predicted[3] and it flies in the face of accepted short-term wisdom.

Of course, away from the macro facts and myths about planetary procreation, there are, it must be said, some fantastically bizarre ones on the micro level too.

For instance, if you need to give your chances of conception a wee boost and in vitro fertilisation (IVF) isn't for you, allow me to offer some alternatives.

Top five fertility rituals from around the world

The Watering of the Girls, Holloko, Hungary

The reality of this ancient event lives up to its ever so slightly worrying name, as young men dressed in traditional Hungarian clothing throw buckets of water over girls to, well, make them wet. Held at Easter and harking back to the area's pre-Christian past, it's become quite the tourist attraction apparently. Take a brolly.

The Mên-an-Tol, Cornwall, United Kingdom

Known locally as the Mên-an-Tol – literally meaning 'the hole stone' in Cornish – it's not hard to see why this Bronze Age monument was given fertility superpowers at some point during its 4,500-year history. Local legend claims that if a woman passes through the stone hole seven times backwards, at a full moon, she will either fall pregnant or fall over.

Kanamara Matsuri, Japan

When it comes to fertility rituals the Japanese don't mess about – and you don't have to go far to find an enormous phallus or two hundred thousand.

Held every year in March, Kanamara Matsuri is based around the story of a demon who dismembered a man as he got to know his wife on their wedding night. It features Shinto priests playing musical instruments, a colourful parade, all the sake you can put away and, of course, penises.

Lots of penises.

Candles, lollies, statues, floats, hats – everything goes totally phallus in the name of fertility and, nowadays, to raise money for HIV research.

The Weeping Column, Istanbul, Turkey

Again, it's hard here to know which came first – the double entendre or the fertility ritual – but worshippers and tourists have been visiting the Weeping Column inside stunning Hagia Sophia for centuries. The column – also known as the Column of St Gregory – is said to weep holy water capable of curing everything from blindness to infertility.

Taken from the Temple of Artemis in Ephesus, the column is made of white marble and now stands in the northern corner of the museum. Visitors place their thumb into a hole in the column and turn it 360 degrees. If their thumb comes out feeling damp, it is said their infertility problems are over.

Cerne Abbas Giant, Dorset, United Kingdom

Among the rolling, lush hills of rural Dorset in the south of England stands a 55 metre high chalk giant sporting what must be one of the biggest erections anywhere on the planet.

The facts surrounding the origins of the Cerne Abbas Giant are flaky to say the least, and despite claims that it is an ancient creation dating back thousands of years it can actually be traced back only to the late seventeenth century. Some believe it was a mockery of military and political leader Oliver Cromwell.

But no matter, with such enormous credentials on show, it stands to reason that local folklore would hold it up as being an aid to fertility, and it is said that any woman who sleeps on the figure will be blessed with children.

Fertility food

In between the folklore of old and the slick science of today, though, there sits a factor that can help us all become parents, no matter where we are or how much money we have – our diet.

The consensus among fertility experts like the UK's Zita West is that food choices are one of the major factors for successful conception.[4]

Adequate protein from lean meat and fish, essential fats from fish, nuts and seeds, wholemeal carbohydrates and copious amounts of fruit and vegetables are the order of the day, with a three-month window of healthy eating needed to see an improvement in egg and sperm quality.

So a salad the night before you try just isn't going to cut it.

For the man, the likes of oily fish for its omega-3 and omega-6 oils, garlic for its selenium and antioxidants, and avocados for vitamin E are key to aid sperm mobility and development.

For women, full-fat dairy is viewed as a must, as is chicken rather than red meat for protein. A Harvard University study[5] found that women who eat at least one serving of full-fat dairy a day reduce their risk of infertility by more than 25% because it's thought that the fat in dairy helps improve the function of the ovaries.

Consuming lots of orange-coloured fruit and veg in particular is said to be a good move because of their high levels of beta-carotene, which the body turns into vitamin A to aid ovulation – all washed down with lashings of water, which works wonders for egg follicles, womb lining and cervical fluid.

An interesting thing happens when you put the list of what modern thinking deems good to eat for fertility next to a rundown of food to which one part of the world or another has attributed aphrodisiacal powers at some point during the past 2,000 years or so.

Again, it's tempting to scoff as you read down a list of what our forefathers considered a good thing to gird the loins. And it's obvious that some of them were included for their aesthetic qualities, shall we say, rather than their powers to actually stimulate physiologically – but there's often much more to what different territories have seen as aphrodisiacs than meets the eye.

Take the avocado, known as the 'testicle tree' by the Aztecs because its pendulous fruit hangs in pairs. But, as we saw earlier, they are also chock full of vitamin E, a key nutrient in sperm development. If the man with the 11 children in your village ate a lot of the green things that hung down like a couple of you-know-whats, that would surely have been enough to give avocados a reputation as the fertility fruit, would it not?

Bananas? Obviously as phallic as it gets, and long thought of as an aphrodisiac, but we also now know that they're rich in potassium and B vitamins, which are said to be necessary for sex hormone production.

Carrots? Ditto on the phallic front and they've been associated with sex for centuries – early Middle Eastern royalty were particularly partial. But aside from its shape, modern nutritionists now know that its high levels of beta-carotene are converted into vitamin A and give ovulation a boost.

Garlic? Tibetan monks were not allowed to enter the monastery if they had been eating garlic, not because their breath was likely to shock a brother or two out of his vow of silence but because of its reputation for stirring up passions. Garlic has now been proven to increase circulation – and we all know what more blood flow can lead to, don't we?

Likewise with sweet basil. For centuries it was believed that the herb stimulated the sex drive and increased fertility. The very scent of it was said to drive men wild – so much so that women would dust their breasts with the stuff. Hey presto (or should that be pesto?), basil has a growing reputation as a circulatory booster too.

Oysters, which have been put in the folder marked 'aesthetic aphrodisiac' because someone somewhere once thought they looked like female genitalia, actually turn out to be high in zinc, a mineral that has been associated with improving sexual potency in men.

Humble liquorice, once a favourite of the Chinese to spark love and lust, has fallen out of favour and is viewed as nothing more than a child's confection these days. That was until a study carried out at the fantastically named Smell and Taste Treatment and Research Foundation in Chicago[6] discovered that the smell of black liquorice increased blood flow to the penis by a sizable 13% – so it looks like the ancients were on to something once again.

It's also worth noting, though, that in the same study the number jumped to 32% when the liquorice smell was combined with that of doughnuts!

Which goes to show that it really does take all sorts.

But perhaps the most intriguing of all the fertility foods at the moment is one of the key ingredients in sea cucumber and *huai shan* congee, a dish recommended by many traditional Chinese medicine practitioners as being an aid to fertility. You might be forgiven for thinking, if your mind has already been contaminated with all this talk of phallic-shaped aphrodisiacs, that the cucumber is the crucial part of this porridge when it comes to baby making. While it is indeed a nutritious beast, it is actually the *huai shan* (or dried yam) that is the most interesting part.

Some 7,000 miles away in south-western Nigeria in a town called Igbo-Ora, a long-occurring phenomenon has been catching the eye of fertility experts. Namely, that 40.2 out of every 1,000 deliveries in the area result in twins – that's more than four times higher than the global average.

Igbo-Ora and its surrounding region is the twin capital of the world. But why?

Yams. That's why.

It turns out that the yam is the absolute staple of the local diet and it has long been thought locally that the root contains a chemical property that stimulates ovulation and can often result in the natural release of two eggs in a single cycle.[7]

Then, of course, there's also the belief in many cultures that certain foods (not to mention colours, positions and timings) can also dictate the gender of the baby too.

Hey boy, hey girl

There was a time not that long ago when trying to predetermine the gender of your unborn baby was a bit of fun.

If you wanted a boy, it was said you should get to it at night-time, preferably when there was a quarter moon in the sky and on an odd rather than an even day of the month.

Likewise, if at all possible, the head of the lady (always a lady) should be pointing north, with the pleasure of the man being of paramount concern. After you're done, the best sleeping position for a boy baby to occur is man to the right, woman – sorry, lady – to the left.

Got all that? Good. If it's a girl you're after, do all that in reverse – if that's anatomically possible, not to mention legal.

The first time much of this appeared in print was in a fifteenth-century French collection of popular beliefs called *The Distaff Gospels*. The book centres on a gathering of women swapping truths about life as they spin yarn – a distaff being a spinning implement.

Among the fantastic gems imparted are that 'when a woman sleeps with her husband and wants to have a boy rather than a girl, she must hold her hands closed while her husband has intercourse with her'.

Also, 'When a pregnant woman carries her child more on her right side, and she enjoys hearing about tournaments and jousts, you should know for certain that she will have a son.'

If she'd rather chat about dances and music, congratulations – it's a girl!

It's worth noting, though, that the gospels also go on to warn that when you see a cat sitting in the sun in a window, licking her behind and not rubbing her ear with her leg, you can be sure that it will rain that very day.

Food for thought for us all, I'm sure you will agree.

Talking of which, there are also the things that diet can tell us, both before and during pregnancy. If you're hoping for a girl, drink lots of milk and water, eat cheese and yoghurt, and go easy on the meat and potatoes.

For a boy, your menu should consist of copious vegetables, with the exception of cress, lettuce, raw cabbage, spinach and cauliflower – which are such obvious exclusions that they barely warrant mentioning really.

Or if you'd rather not tweak what you eat to determine your baby's gender, why not simply put a wooden spoon under your bed and a pink ribbon under your pillow to bring the pitter-patter of female feet – which is second only to shouting out of the window 'I WANT A GIRL' on the Ronseal scale.

It's worth sparing a thought for some Hispanic mothers-to-be, who can be blasted with a triple whammy on the food for thought front. First, if they suffer heartburn while carrying their baby – which many do, of course – their baby will be hairy. Very, very hairy.

Eating fruit, something that as a pregnant woman you'd be forgiven for thinking would be risk free, is also said to come at a cost –'dirty' babies. Then, to top it all, cheese and dairy are to be avoided too, lest you want your newborn to be struck down with chronic cradle cap.

In the 1960s and 1970s things got a little more scientific, with two theories from the USA that seemed to make a bit more sense at least.

First, there was the Shettles Method. This stated that sperm bearing a Y chromosome (for boys) move faster but don't live as long as sperm that carry X chromosomes (for girls). So if you want a boy, the Shettles Method contends, you should have sex as close as possible to ovulation. If you want a girl, you should have sex two to four days before you ovulate.

Then we have the Whelan Method, which handily contradicts everything about the Shettles Method and advises you to have sex four to six days before the lady's basal body temperature spikes if you want to conceive a boy, and two to three days before you ovulate if you want a girl.

What all of the above rather gloriously have in common, no matter where they originate, no matter how plausible or otherwise they may sound, is that they are all a load of old rubbish.

Charming? Perhaps. In any way useful? No.

But never fear! As is the way of things, science has stepped in to fill the folklore void with high-tech gender selection.

Procedures such as preimplantation genetic diagnosis were originally developed to help couples who have gone through genetic testing and know they are carriers of serious gender-linked disorders. Often termed 'family balancing', this is now being used in conjunction with IVF to determine the sex of an embryo for those with the burning desire – and mountains of cash – to do it.

Of course, only embryos of the desired sex will be implanted in the uterus, which is why most fertility centres discourage it if there is no real medical reason to select gender.

All of which makes the wooden spoon under the bed seem a somehow more attractive proposition, even if it does result in the fifty–fifty status quo.

Where fertility is concerned, it really does seem that, as science makes advances, we not only lose a global perspective but also see generations of tradition tossed aside in an instant.

When clinicians get involved, they tend to make things very clinical.

The fertility franchise

I f there's a more intense, anxious or emotionally charged place to be than the waiting room of an IVF clinic, I'm all for giving it a miss.

Having experienced the IVF world, more correctly termed assisted reproductive technology (ART), I now look on in awe and admiration at those who spend years at the conception coalface.

As we'll see, the financial toll that assisted fertility treatment takes varies from country to country, but no matter where you are it's never cheap. Where the most damage is done, though, is undoubtedly on the physical and emotional front, as increasing numbers of women the world over put themselves through hell for the baby they crave. The self-injecting, hormonal onslaught, constant fear of failure and all-consuming despair that comes if things don't work out combine to represent a display of our fundamental desire to procreate – so determined and strong that it genuinely takes the breath away to witness it at close quarters.

Is this rise in fertility issues and the treatment of them a global phenomenon? And is it handled the same way everywhere? Has the fertility business industrialised conception in the West for good?

Let's find out.

The rise and rise of IVF

People often glibly tell you that having a baby is a blessing.

They are right, of course, but occasionally in the first year or so, normally at 3.56a.m., you'll find yourself walking around your living room with a wide awake and windy little bundle and raise an eyebrow, if you can muster the energy, in the direction of that sentiment.

But the moment someone tells you that your ability to have a child is in doubt, the yearning begins, and it's that which is written on the faces of each and every person you meet during the IVF journey – and you meet a staggering number of them.

A combination of factors led by the fact that women are having children later in the West – and even increasingly in burgeoning economies like China – has seen the spread of IVF clinics rival even the charge of the coffee and burger chains when it comes to geographical spread.

It's an astonishing story of a branch of medicine that simply didn't exist 35 years ago. In fact, research into the field began in the USA as early as the 1930s, when scientists at Harvard attempted in vitro fertilisation on rabbits – as if they needed any help in that direction.

In the 1940s, unsuccessful assisted reproductive techniques were attempted using human eggs – and again in the mid-1960s researchers at Johns Hopkins University tried to fertilise *in vitro* (which comes from the Latin for 'in glass').

But it wasn't until Louise Brown's momentous birth in the English town of Oldham on 25 July 1978 that IVF as we know it today came into being.

The world's media may have immediately termed the 5 pound 12 ounce (2.608kg) little girl as the 'test tube baby', but her conception, like the astonishing 5 million IVF babies it is estimated have followed her, actually took place in a petri dish.

It was a while, though, before the trickle turned into a flood, and a slow stream of similar scientific triumphs in Australia in 1980, the USA in 1981 and Sweden and France in 1982 followed before momentum gathered, expertise began to spread and the IVF revolution really kicked off in earnest.

In the early days, those wanting to go down the IVF route were required to spend two to three weeks in hospital and had to keep all of their urine during the treatment for analysis because it was the only way doctors could keep track of hormone levels. Of course, it's easily forgotten now just how intense the media interest was in this new-fangled baby-making technique back then. Women undergoing treatment were routinely warned not to talk to the media, to be wary of phone enquiries and to avoid mentioning the names of women they'd met at the clinic.

With success rates in the early years averaging at around 10%, the overwhelming chances were that all the effort would turn out to be in vain, but that didn't deter couples from around the world signing up and driving the innovation and research that turned assisted fertility into the multi-billion-pound industry it is today.

There may be no constant urine collection for those undergoing ART nowadays, and no journalists desperate to know the details, but while assisted conception numbers continue to increase from continent to continent, it remains far from being a straightforward undertaking to have a baby via artificial means. Each clinic differs, of course, but women are now treated as day patients pretty much across the board. The trade-off is that they are required to self-administer their own ovarian stimulation drugs.

And by administer I mean inject. To watch your partner stab herself with not insubstantial sized needles three times a day so you can both have a baby is a sobering experience indeed.

And the numbers of women putting themselves through it are staggering. The World Health Organization estimates that there are between 120 million and 160 million couples struggling with infertility worldwide.

Although one wide-ranging report[8] has suggested that levels of infertility were similar in 2010 to those a decade earlier in 1990, it's estimated that one in six couples across the planet experience some form of infertility problem at least once during their reproductive lifetime. Around 20% to 30% of infertility cases are explained by physiological causes in men, 20% to 35% by physiological causes in women, and 25% to 40% of cases are because of a problem in both partners. In 10% to 20%, a diagnosis of 'unexplained infertility' is given.

While links have been made between infertility and lifestyle factors such as smoking, body weight and stress, by far the single most referenced reason for the general rise in infertility across the globe is the increasing age of the female partner, with the vast majority of assisted fertility treatments carried out worldwide taking place in women aged between 30 and 39.

In the UK and Germany, the average age of the first-time mother has tipped over 30 for the first time, according to the Organisation for Economic Co-operation and Development (OECD),[9] with a swathe of other countries about to follow suit. That represents an astonishing social shift given that just a generation or so ago there were many, many more new mothers below 25 than there were above it.

While this change arguably brings with it many socio-economic and gender equality benefits, there's no doubt that it is also fuelling an assisted fertility revolution. In 2010, the year for which the latest figures are available, 147,260 IVF cycles were carried out in the US, 61,774 across Australia and New Zealand, 79,427 in France, 74,672 in Germany and around 59,000 in each of Italy, Spain and the UK.[10]

Away from the raw numbers, and in terms of cycles per head of population, the Nordic and Low Countries are setting the pace with more than 3% of all babies born conceived via artificial means.

Conspicuous by its absence in many of the official IVF figures is China, but that doesn't mean there isn't a burgeoning IVF industry in the world's fastest-growing economy – far from it, in fact.

Given the extreme measures China has famously taken to slow its population growth, this might surprise some, but after China's first IVF baby was born in 1988 the Beijing government was supportive of IVF. By the mid-1990s there was a subtle but very real shift from every family being able to have only one child to every family being given the chance to have one child.

In 2001, there were five private ART centres in mainland China, a figure that has now risen to well over 200 and looks set to grow further. The strength of the Chinese government's backing of assisted reproduction was demonstrated in 2008 when treatment was offered to the parents of the 7,000 children who lost their lives in the devastating earthquake that struck the country.

Perhaps understandably there's much media debate in China about the propensity of ART to produce multiple births and its use as a way of circumventing the one-child policy. If that's the case it's an expensive solution, because in China – as in almost every other country in the world – assisted fertility treatment remains hugely expensive relative to average incomes.

In fact, such are the costs involved that one leading fertility expert, Lord Robert Winston, a pioneer in the field who has served as a scientific adviser to the World Health Organization's programme in human reproduction, has brought into question not just some of the claims made by private clinics about their success rates, but also the amount of money being charged by many of them, going as far as labelling some in the sector as exploitative.[11]

As a result of these cost issues, assisted fertility treatment tourism has become very big business – an estimated 20,000 to 25,000 couples go abroad each year to take advantage of assisted reproductive technology services.[12]

Fertility far and wide

Those choosing to take flight in a bid to keep costs down are increasingly looking east or to emerging nations. Travelling with a US dollar, pound or euro in your pocket to places such as India, South Korea, Thailand, Spain and Turkey, which offer high-quality treatment for often a fraction of the cost they would pay at home, is fast becoming a go-to option for couples either priced out of the market or whose unsuccessful attempts in their native countries have cleaned out their savings.

As more and more cities market themselves as ART destinations, complete with shiny websites offering the full five-star fluffy towel service, what's emerging is that people's ability to traverse the complicated international latticework of ART regulations is also becoming a major driver in who goes where and why – as well as cost.

For a mixture of religious, moral and cultural reasons, ART remains a controversial and morally divisive medical practice and individual questions around issues such as the use of donor eggs or the freezing of spare embryos for future use have created sizable regulatory disparities between states.

Perhaps the most geographically variable issue of all is the number of embryos allowed to be transferred back into the woman in each territory. Although it's true to say that there is a consistent global trend towards fewer embryos than in previous decades – the worldwide average is estimated to stand currently at 1.75 embryos per transfer – it is still a deeply contentious question that sees thousands travelling across the globe to access what they see as a game-changing advantage.

In Europe, figures from 2010 show that the multiple delivery rate per embryo transfer has declined steadily since 2000 from 26.9% to 19.2%, whereas in the US, where legislation has been at its most lax, the multiple delivery rate is significantly higher at 33%.

Take a traditionally Catholic country like Poland and you see how these issues begin to become not just morally problematic but governmentally troublesome too.

It's not that ART is illegal – in fact, thousands of Polish couples have paid for treatment across the country's 50 or so clinics – but the entire branch of artificial reproductive medicine is in many ways unrecognised and therefore unregulated. And that means there's little or no oversight of the disposal of unused embryos.

This in turn has led to Poland's powerful bishops consistently and vociferously opposing bills that have been tabled to bring IVF under some sort of state regulatory umbrella. The bishops have called IVF treatment the 'younger sister of eugenics' and one archbishop even went as far as to say that MPs who supported any of the bills that did not ban IVF outright would be excommunicated.

At the other end of the spectrum, Israel is one of the leading fertility tourism destinations and has the highest number of fertility clinics per capita on the planet. The aforementioned liberal legislative approach in many US states also drives strong European traffic across the Atlantic, with those wanting to play the numbers game and put back multiple embryos tempted to make the journey and pay the money.

And, wherever you are, it is big money. But does it need to be?

The future of IVF?

Calculating the cost of an IVF cycle is not a straightforward business. While the core costs are often stated up front, the variable blood tests, scans and often huge drug costs can all be added in to make for a truly frightening overall total.

What's more, not only is the difference in cost across different territories vast, but there's no simple way of making informed financial decisions about where to go for treatment – short of researching each and every clinic in each and every country on a case-by-case basis, that is. What may cost you £15,000 in the USA, Hong Kong or the UK, may set you back only £3,000 in the Czech Republic, South Korea or India.

For something so emotionally charged and important to those going through it, the lack of internationally coordinated regulation around pricing as well as technique is a problem that feels like it will get much worse before it gets better.

At least in the area of charges, though, there could be a white knight on the horizon in the form of some pioneering and blissfully simple work done by a team from the Genk Institute for Fertility Technology.

Put simply, the Belgian team has cut the frills and therefore the cost too. Whereas conventional IVF labs use expensive incubators in rooms with purified air and sophisticated systems and kit to aid in the selection and screening of embryos, the Genk approach is to go back to basics and essentially create austerity IVF!

So instead of pumping pricey medical-grade carbon dioxide into the incubator, they discovered that you could happily generate the gas by dissolving an Alka-Seltzer in water or by mixing kitchen cupboard-grade baking soda with citric acid.

As for the incubator itself, why not make one out of two 7p tubes with rubber stoppers, with the carbon dioxide made in the first and transferred to the second. The eggs and sperm are then injected into the second tube, where, all being well, fertilisation occurs. The rubber stoppers keep everything airtight, removing the need for purified air, and after three to five days the embryos are then ready to transfer to the woman's womb.

It's wine making meets baby making.

This isn't some pie in the sky garden shed hypothesis of an experiment either. The Belgian team has actually used this homespun method, and by mid-2013 they already had 12 healthy babies as a result of it. Their success rate of 30% is approximately the same as IVF, but the projected cost – now that's very different indeed – just £170 per cycle!

If this technique becomes widely available, it won't just vastly reduce the financial burden for those who are already considering ART treatment, it will also make it an option for the millions of infertile couples in the developing world who are currently priced out of trying for the baby they long for.

So we've seen the distinct approaches of myths and medicine where infertility is concerned, but there is a treatment that has uniquely managed to span the divide between East and West, old and new.

The need for needles

On the face of it there's nothing less likely to be accepted by the medical profession as a sound and worthwhile treatment for fertility than sticking tiny needles in various parts of your body.

It's not even as if the needles are brimming with the various hormones like the ones that most IVF patients have to self-administer as they transform themselves into human pincushions during the course of their treatment.

No, acupuncture should, by rights, be thrown casually into the bin marked crackpot garbage by the planet's medicalised fertility specialists, where it can nestle alongside all the other practices that they consider to be hokum, like homeopathy, aromatherapy and sticking your legs in the air after intercourse to speed the sperm up a bit (it doesn't make a blind bit of difference, apparently).[13]

The thing is, though, that over the past couple of decades the white coats of the West seem not only to have begrudgingly recognised what the East's ancient tradition of acupuncture can achieve when it comes to fertility, but in many cases to actively promote it now too.

The traditional belief is that by stimulating specific acupuncture points a correction occurs of an imbalance in the flow of 'qi' – the life force or energy that forms the underlying principle in traditional Chinese medicine, and, for that matter, in most martial arts – flowing through a complex network of channels, or 'meridians', around the body.

Unsurprisingly, for the world of modern medicine, that's quite a lot to swallow. But a seemingly more palatable theory has emerged as a potential explanation of how acupuncture works specifically around fertility – namely that it stimulates the autonomic nervous system, which helps to control muscles and glands, and makes the lining of the uterus more receptive to receiving an embryo.

Perhaps more important than the debate around *how* acupuncture works is the question of *if* it works. There can't have been a time since its inception in ancient China thousands of years ago when the practice has been so keenly studied and measured – yet despite the focus and scrutiny we are still none the wiser, and each study seems to contradict the last.

In 2008, for instance, we had researchers at the University of Maryland School of Medicine in the US and the VU University Amsterdam declaring that women having acupuncture while undergoing IVF increase their chances of getting pregnant by an enormous 65%.[14]

A total of 1,366 women undergoing IVF were included in the trials – the women were of differing ages and suffering from differing infertility issues. The researchers compared acupuncture given within one day of embryo transfer, sham acupuncture where needles were inserted away from points used in genuine acupuncture, and no additional treatment, and they discovered a 65% uplift in pregnancy for those who had been given the genuine needle treatment.

Then, just two years later in 2010, the headlines lurched the other way with the British Fertility Society warning patients that there was zero evidence that acupuncture (or the use of Chinese traditional herbs for that matter) helps conception, after a scientific review of 14 previous studies from around the world involving 2,670 women.[15]

So that was that. Conclusive clinical proof that acupuncture is a waste of time and money – until the next study was released in 2012, of course, which showed a positive effect on IVF outcomes to a statistically significant level,[16] only for a Cochrane Review to again find no evidence of the sort a few months later in July 2013.[17]

I'll stop now, but you get the picture. After a blizzard of studies it still ostensibly remains the case that the use of acupuncture in IVF treatment is down to personal belief. How much can actually be drawn from the ever increasing number of IVF clinics prepared to recommend it as a complementary and worthwhile treatment is debatable. Is there bandwagon jumping going on there, or perhaps – even more darkly – is it just another way for money to be made from people who are so desperate for a baby that the thought of failing because they didn't try this or that is just too much to bear?

As ever, in the world of parenting the hard and fast answer is a tantalisingly elusive beast and what may seem initially straightforward soon becomes multidimensional and downright devilish on closer inspection.

Luckily, though, we are about to move on to look at a period of serenity and joy that is the prelude to perhaps the most natural of all moments in any of our lives – what could we possibly learn from each other about pregnancy and birth?

Lots.

....

A parent's perspective

Jane – UK and Spain

Our path to family life has been a long one. It's hard now to remember that it nearly didn't happen and even harder not to take it for granted.

I met my now husband when we were both in our mid-thirties and I knew that time wasn't on my side fertility-wise, but I am married to Mr Positive who didn't doubt we'd end up as parents, and the slightly eccentric way that we have got there now just seems right for us.

After two unsuccessful attempts at intrauterine insemination (IUI) – essentially a medicalised turkey baster courtesy of the NHS, there followed three rounds of IVF at our huge expense (our particular health authority didn't fund IVF if you are over 35). After changing clinics and yet more tests, we were finally told that my eggs were not of good enough quality for IVF to work and were given a less than 5% chance of another round working.

Egg donation was suggested and we were told that it was easier and quicker to go abroad, with Spain being mentioned as a particularly good option.

After a momentary mourning for my pickled eggs and the end of my genes, we soon actually warmed to the idea pretty quickly. We had looked into adoption, but had put that off as being a challenge we didn't feel ready for, so egg donation was an easier leap of faith. I would get to be pregnant and give birth, we both love Spain and my father-in-law lives there, so we booked a holiday to check out some clinics.

In the end we only went to see two clinics and, although both were brilliant, we went for a small clinic in Marbella, close to family ties. We met with the friendly consultant and the English nurses and for the first time since our fertility became medicalised, we were treated like individuals. They have plenty of young donors, who get paid 900 euros – enough to be compensated but not enough to go through with it just for the money (I hope) and they are anonymous.

It's so weird that the only things we know about the incredible woman whose (too tiny for the human eye to see) eggs eventually became our amazing children is that she was 26, worked in a shop, liked dancing, swimming and reading. We love her and will tell the twins when they are old enough that they have a Spanish fairy godmother.

Yes, twins!

OK, it took three tries and one wasted trip because a donor hadn't responded to the stimulation drug, but we ended up with twins who are now three and look like their dad but with deliciously olive skin, love dancing, swimming and reading, and are learning Spanish watching Dora the Explorer. *I always loved Spain and now we have even more excuses to spend time there.*

Our children feel 100% like our children but we'd like to share with them the story of their incredible journey getting to us and show them the country that is a little part of who they are.

WORLDLY WISDOM - FERTILITY

The World Health Organization estimates that there are between 120 million and 160 million couples struggling with infertility worldwide.

In the UK and Germany the average age of the first-time mother is now over 30 for the first time.

India, Spain, South Korea, Thailand and Turkey offer some of the cheapest high-quality IVF treatment on the planet.

Fifty years ago the average global fertility rate was five children per female. Today it is just 2.5.

2
Pregnancy and birth

Baby on board
Is there a pregnancy heaven?

How long does a pregnancy last?

Congratulations. You're pregnant.

You'd imagine, despite the myriad of myths, traditions and differing practices that surround almost everything to do with having a baby, one thing would be indisputable no matter where you called home.

Namely that for us humans, a full-term, on-time pregnancy lasts nine months.

Not in Japan it doesn't.

In the land where order is everything, a pregnancy lasts a tidy 10 months, not an ungainly and awkward nine. The rationale behind this is that the months are counted as exactly 28 days. Since actual months vary from 28 to 31 days, nine calendar months are equal to 10 months of 28 days.

Clear? Good.

What this means is that there is no debate about when each trimester begins and things are simple, straightforward and logical – the first trimester (*ninshin shoki*) lasts for the first four months, the second trimester (*ninshin chuuki*) lasts from month five to month seven, and the third (*ninshin kouki*) from the eighth to the tenth.

(Once the big moment finally does arrive, the presence of the father at the birth is perfectly acceptable for the vast majority of Japanese maternity hospitals, so long as he stays put by his wife's head and never ventures to the business end of things at any point in the proceedings in case he is traumatised by what he sees!)

The French also have their own way of calculating the gestation period.

In the US and UK, for example, the due date is calculated by counting 40 weeks from the first day of the woman's last menstrual cycle, including two weeks until conception and 38 weeks of gestation.

In France, doctors calculate the due date by starting two weeks from the first day of the woman's last menstrual cycle and then count on nine months. That equates to two weeks until conception and 39 weeks of gestation – resulting in 41 weeks of pregnancy.

But once the due date has been decided on, it's plain sailing all the way to the delivery for mothers everywhere.

Well, not quite, of course.

There are one or two (hundred) different beliefs to negotiate first depending on where you are.

If you're in Bali, avoid eating octopus as it leads to a difficult delivery – probably because of all those arms.

Bolivian? Under no circumstances knit clothes for your little bun in the oven as it can cause the umbilical cord to wrap around the baby's neck.

Inuit? Avoid inflating balloons or blowing bubblegum bubbles for fear they will rupture membranes.

Elsewhere, the award for most pampered and lovingly protected pregnant women in the world goes to Polynesia, where they are often nurtured by the entire community throughout the duration of their gestational period. In addition to this communal sense of caretaking, a midwife visits regularly to administer massages!

In fact, in Maori culture fathers are taught how to do a special Maori pregnancy massage that utilises a combination of gentle stomach massage, body alignment and pressure points – and they're advised to do it as often as possible for the benefit of both the *whaea* (mother) and *peepi* (baby).

(If there's a cuter name for a baby than *peepi* anywhere on the planet I've not been lucky enough to come across it.)

Chinese mothers-to-be should steer clear of evil spirits, funerals and sex – and if all three are encountered at the same venue it is to be treated as a matter for the police.

The personality of an unborn child is also thought in Chinese tradition to be strongly influenced by the state of his mother's mind and body while expecting. For this reason, Chinese women are strongly urged to avoid gossiping, temper tantrums and physical labour too.

A similar belief in Korea has been given a slightly different twist, with mothers needing to take in as much beauty and feel as much positivity as they can while pregnant. The more joy they imbibe the more gorgeous their baby will be. This even extends to them avoiding any breakable foods like cookies or crackers for fear they will make their baby sick, and they don't eat duck so their kids won't have webbed feet.

While the 'hoisin pancake equals ugly duckling' link is perhaps taking things a bit too far, modern science has proved the Chinese and Korean traditions around the mother's state of mind having a direct impact on the baby to have more than a little validity.

A host of studies[18] have found that stress during pregnancy in particular has been linked to a shorter gestation and higher incidence of preterm birth, an increased risk of miscarriage, and problems with the child's attention and emotional reactivity in later life.

That's quite a list and means that, as is often the case, a belief that is all too easy to view as an ancient wives' tale is actually true at its core.

For the majority of mothers today, though, it's true to say there are two issues that dominate when it comes to the potential to create anxiety and stress. One is as old as birth itself and the other is a very modern phenomenon.

The pain game

As the reality of labour approaches, the pain of childbirth and how to manage it loom large for many women.

It's not only the way in which the pain itself is dealt with that differs globally, it's the very perception of it too.

In some cultures, particularly in parts of Asia, how a woman handles labour pains has traditionally been seen to reflect upon her family's honour, while in Mediterranean cultures a far more expressive and emotional approach is taken, with mothers giving birth with clear and expressive communication of how they're feeling.[19]

Or so the cultural stereotypes go.

But is pain just pain wherever you are? Individuals might have different pain thresholds, but entire cultures? Does being stoic when pain relief just isn't available a cause or an effect?

There's no easy answer to any of those questions and, as we will explore later, the increasing spread of medicalised labour throws up much to debate.

And, of course, opinions abound, with one of the most controversial in recent years coming from one of the UK's most influential midwives – who just happens to be a man.

Dr Denis Walsh suggested that women should endure the agony of labour because pain-relieving drugs, including epidural injections, not only carry serious medical risks but also diminish childbirth as a rite of passage and undermine the mother's bond with her child.[20]

That's quite a claim – and one that provoked widespread fury, as well as some support.

Arguing that women avoid experiencing the discomfort of childbirth because hospital maternity staff are too quick to offer an epidural is one thing, going on to say that pain in labour is a purposeful, useful thing and prepares a mother for the responsibility of nurturing a new-born baby is quite another.

That feels very close to suggesting that having your leg amputated without an anaesthetic is a smart long-term move because it prepares you for life on one foot being quite a trial!

What is beyond argument is the fact that the worldwide use of epidurals as pain management in childbirth is spiralling. Although country-by-country statistics for the procedure are surprisingly sketchy, a robust survey carried out in 2008 in the United States showed that 61% of women who gave birth vaginally had epidural or spinal anaesthesia – with other estimates putting the number as high as 80% in some states. Surveys also show a third of Australian mothers using it too, a quarter of those in Britain, and in hotspots across Europe as many as 98% calling for the needle.[21]

Although an epidural is the most common type of pain medication used by labouring women in the US, nitrous oxide, or 'laughing gas', is far more popular elsewhere – it's used by 60% of women in labour in the United Kingdom, 50% in Australia and almost 50% who deliver in Finland and Canada.[22]

Despite being around since 1881 and being able to be self-administered since 1934, the technique, which doesn't so much stop the pain as distract labouring mothers from it, has never really broken America.

For many around the world, of course, the debate about what's safe and what's best is irrelevant because there's just no pain relief available.

Over time there has been a myriad of ways of approaching the pain of childbirth. Guatemalan women, for instance, believe that speedy delivery can be induced by drinking a liquid created by boiling a purple onion in beer – whereas in Morocco the midwife massages the stomach and vulva with olive oil to make the baby's passage easier.

But if there's one thing that can possibly rival the worry that impending labour brings it's the financial pressure which comes with being a modern working, earning woman who is about to have a baby.

Maternity leave

For millions of modern mothers across the world there is one practical issue above almost all others that clouds the horizon as pregnancy progresses – that of maternity benefit.

Depending on where they find themselves, the financial cover they will receive once the baby arrives can either be a huge calming relief, a source of gut-wrenching worry or, in some cases, pretty much non-existent.

Maternity benefits provided for the birth or adoption of a baby vary from country to country and not always in the way you'd imagine. Here's a quiz question to demonstrate.

What has the United States got in common with Papua New Guinea, Swaziland, Liberia and Lesotho?

I can accept 'not much on the face of it' as your final answer if you'd like, but you might want to reconsider.

The United States, the planet's richest single nation, is joined together with four of the very poorest in not legally requiring companies to offer some type of paid maternity leave for its new mothers.[23]

In at least 178 other countries paid leave is guaranteed, to a greater or lesser degree, for those mothers who need to work – which is, of course, a growing number of them. In most of those countries, women on maternity leave are guaranteed between 75% and 100% of their salary, according to the International Labour Organization's study *Maternity Protection at Work*.[24]

But for most in the United States they get zip, and the crippling loss of income leads to many American couples struggling with the financial impact of having a child and often sees necessities being charged to credit cards and a spiral of debt beginning.

There are some notable corporate exceptions in the US – many of the Silicon Valley giants are moving to stop what they had noticed was a flood of female talent leaving organisations because of the lack of attractive maternity cover on offer.

In response, Google increased its maternity package from three months to five months and changed its pay policy to give new mothers full pay throughout that time. (They also give employees $500 for takeout food to help out in the first gruelling weeks!) As a result, the number of women leaving decreased by half.

But even that increased package pales against the best the rest of the world has to offer.

As we will come to see often on our journey around Planet Parent, it's the Scandinavian countries that come out on top. Sweden, for instance, offers up to 80% of the average wage for a whopping 480 days and Norway pays up to 100% of wages for 42–52 weeks, with the Danes proffering a similar deal with up to 100% of wages for a year.

But it's not just the Scandis who set the pace when it comes to this. Eastern Europe isn't doing badly either, with Croatia, Serbia and

Bosnia and Herzegovina all providing up to 100% of wages for an entire year.

Even Albania, once viewed as one of the least progressive nations on the face of the earth, provides its new mothers with up to 80% of their wages for 52 weeks.

But maternity leave isn't just about mothers; studies have shown that its length and quality also strongly impacts on the rest of a child's life.

A report by Save the Children found that in countries with longer periods of maternity leave, children were breastfed for longer and had a higher life expectancy.[25]

So we know the length of time a new-born baby gets to spend with its mother is financially important, depends on geography and is even crucial developmentally – but what about fathers? Where in the world do they get treated best when it comes to spending time with their newborn?

Parental leave

When the British government announced that from April 2015 both parents will be able to share 12 months of leave after the birth of a child, it was heralded – at least by the politicians who announced it – as a groundbreaking piece of progressive public policy making.

And it *was* groundbreaking, for Britain at least.

The Swedish – yes, them again – have had the same law in place since 1974.

1974!

There's being forward thinking and there's being downright annoying. The policy, as with similar ones in Norway and Iceland, sees a 'daddy quota' adopted. Unlike in the UK, where a couple decides how they share their time off, the Scandinavian system reserves part of the parental leave period exclusively for fathers in a 'use it or lose it' model designed to tempt fathers to stay at home and women back to the workplace.

Despite the odd difference in exactly how it is administered, shared or paid paternal leave is now on the statute books of many European countries. Germany perhaps is among the most generous, with new parents able to take up to 14 months of parental leave on 65% of their salary. Then there's Spain, offering four weeks of paid paternity leave as well as 300 weeks of legally sanctioned parental leave after the birth of a new baby to be shared between a couple until their child is three years old.

But elsewhere around the world it's a very different picture for fathers.

The economic powerhouses of China and India, for example, allow no leave, paid or unpaid, shared or otherwise for fathers at all. As we've seen, the United States is a tough place to be a new mother where leave is concerned, and dads don't fair much better – there's no paid parental leave and a maximum of 12 weeks' unpaid parental leave for mothers and fathers.

Many fathers across Africa get no paternity leave at all, the main exceptions being Kenya, which offers two weeks, and Cameroon, Chad, Gabon and Côte d'Ivoire, which allow 10 days. South African fathers get a pretty slim three days to bond with their newborn and help their partner recover from labour.

The good news from down under is that the leave available to be shared between mothers and fathers in Australia is plentiful at a generous 52 weeks. The bad news is it's all unpaid.

What's more, an astonishing survey a decade ago found a direct link between very early interaction between a father and his baby and long-term mental well-being for the child.

The 14-year-long study by a London-based psychologist found that problems, including significant friendship-building issues in teenagers, could be traced back to a lack of quality time with their fathers in the early months of life.[26]

Planet Birth
The story of pushing, from place to place

The history of birth

For an act so utterly fundamental to our survival, giving birth has a remarkably chequered history no matter where you happen to have found yourself on the planet.

While on average there has been a general downward trajectory of maternal and infant mortality rates across the globe, the statistics, as ever, paint an imperfect picture. The lot of the labouring mother may have become mathematically safer across the board, but there remain huge geographical and cultural differences in how babies get from being in there to being out here.

From the almost total medicalisation of labour in much of the West and beyond, to the truly ancient post-birth traditions that are still alive and well in many countries today, birth remains a controversial and complicated topic that we're still divided about as a species.

Let's start at the beginning . . .

There's hardly a venue, situation or moment in time that hasn't seen the birth of a human baby these past two or three hundred thousand years or so.

Fields, prisons, stables (lots of stables), airplanes, markets – where there have been people, there have been other little people being born. There was even a boy born aboard the *Mayflower*, named, naturally, Oceanus.

As is often the way, the ancient Egyptians provide perhaps the first records of what we would recognise as a birth practice or ritual. The delivery often took place on the relative cool of the house roof or another structure designed to combat the stultifying heat, with a mattress, headrest, mat, cushion and stool arranged in the area.

At delivery, only female helpers were present, not physicians. As we will see, this is something that by and large remained the case pretty much everywhere throughout the centuries and up until very recently indeed.

Another part of the birthing picture that the ancient Egyptians had in place and that lasted until just a few hundred years ago was that women delivered their babies kneeling, or sitting on their heels, or on a delivery seat – and we know this because the hieroglyphic for birth is of a woman squatting, not lying on her back, legs in the air, trying to defy gravity by pushing a baby up and out.

We will come to the part Louis XIV did or didn't play in that shift a bit later on.

Another innovation to have originated around that period, and thought by some to have become popular as a way of making childbirth easier to bear, was belly dancing. Performed by women in honour of the giver of life, the Great Mother, it also acted as a way to strengthen vital muscles ahead of birth. The labouring mother would also squat low and bear down as she rolled her abdominal muscles during labour, with the contractions of the dancing movements strengthening her stomach. According to many who still to this day advocate it before and even during birth, belly dancing can lead to an easier delivery.[27]

Birthing stools, belly dancing and useful hieroglyphics – the Egyptians were all over childbirth in a way that puts many a civilisation since to shame. So far ahead of their time were they, in fact, that one of their scribes had this advice for children everywhere:

> *'Repay your mother for all her care. Give her as much bread as she needs, and carry her as she carried you, for you were a heavy burden to her. When you were finally born, she still carried you on her neck and for three years she suckled you and kept you clean.'*

Which makes that tea cosy on Mother's Day look pretty ordinary, doesn't it?

Having said that, the best they could do to entice the post-birth placenta out was to sing: 'Come down, placenta, come down! I am Horus who conjures in order that she who is giving birth becomes better than she was, as if she was already delivered.'

Which isn't ideal.

Jump a few thousand years forward and what did the Greeks bring to the placental party?

In the main, birth remained an all-woman affair, but a few male healers who were trained in the newly developed Hippocratic approach, which relied on careful observation, deduction and record keeping, also started to appear.

Soranus – one can only presume there was no pun intended – a renowned writer on all things gynaecological in the first century AD, put together a list of preparations for a 'normal' labour that not only wouldn't be out of place today but actually displays an eye for real care rather than the merely medical, a complaint often heard from modern mothers today:

> 'For normal labour one must prepare beforehand: olive
> oil, warm water, warm fomentations, soft sea sponges,
> pieces of wool, bandages, a pillow, things to smell, a
> midwife's stool or chair, two beds, and a proper room. Oil
> for injection and lubrication; warm water in order that the
> parts may be cleansed; warm fomentations for alleviation
> of the pains; sea sponges for sponging off; pieces of wool
> in order that the woman's parts be covered, bandages that
> the newborn may be swaddled; a pillow that the infant
> may be placed upon it below the parturient woman, till the
> afterbirth has also been taken care of; and things to smell
> (such as pennyroyal, a clod of earth, barley groats, as
> well as an apple and a quince and, if the season permits, a
> lemon, a melon, and a cucumber, [and] everything similar
> to these) to revive the labouring woman.'[28]

The campaign to make quince and super-soft sea sponges available to every labouring woman on the planet starts here.

It wasn't all citrus fruit and smelling salts, mind you; the Greeks had moved on from trying to coax a retained placenta out by song and had turned to using counterweights that yanked it out forcibly. While herbal pain relief did exist, it was used only in very complicated births, the pain of a normal labour being seen as a good thing, as part of the process, to be endured not circumnavigated – a view which, as we still see, has its proponents today.

When labour began, a birthing stool was used and the mother crouched over it as the midwife massaged her stomach, while another waited below ready to catch the baby – a vital position that was taken up by midwives for centuries until, it is claimed, the medical profession, and particularly the men who dominated it, found a way of changing the birthing position to stop them having to do the sometimes messy floor work.

What did the Romans ever do for childbirth, I hear you ask?

Well, as it turns out, not much, as they often looked to the Greeks for their medical expertise. Soranus, he of the gynaecological advice and inadvertently apt perineal name, moved to Rome and became the best birth doctor in town.

There are tales that the word 'caesarean' possibly derives from Julius Caesar, because it is thought the great man himself was delivered that way. What's much more likely is that it comes from the Latin word *caedere*, meaning 'to cut' – but that's nowhere near as historically interesting, so we'll pretend we haven't heard it and move on.

What's more factually certain is that Roman C-sections were generally performed to rescue a baby from a dying or already dead mother, and even that the Jewish community in ancient Rome were carrying out C-sections on living mothers who were not in danger and – pretty remarkably given the knowledge and kit available to them at the time – not killing everyone involved when they did so.

All in all, though, things were moving in the right direction with the Romans having taken the best of what the Greeks had learned and working out that dirt was, well, dirty and infection a big killer.

Then, in the fourth century, it all went very wrong, depending on where you found yourself.

As the Roman Empire split in two, the western half was overrun by Germanic types and an awful lot of knowledge, including most Greek and Roman medicine and surgical skill, was forgotten, lost and debunked.

In the eastern half of the Roman Empire, though, Islamic scholars put on the medical mantle and in the ninth century Hunayn ibn Ishaq took all the Greek medical books he could lay his hands on to Baghdad and translated them into Arabic. Muslim medicine flourished for centuries, with hospitals established and advances made.

But childbirth in the Middle Ages in most of Europe became so horrifically risky that heavily pregnant women were encouraged to confess their sins before labour, and midwives, such as they were, had the dubious privilege of being the only laypeople allowed to baptise newborns, so many tragic fatalities did they encounter.[29] It's estimated that one in every three adult women died during their child-bearing years during the darkest of the Dark Ages.

Despite the schism between East and West when it came to medicine and this great cultural and geographical rift, the core practice of birth remained the same. Children were still born at home with the mother being attended to by a local midwife and group of female friends, with no men allowed anywhere near the proceedings – and that included doctors.

The exclusion of the medical men from births may well have been for the best, though. The theory that dominated all Western medicine until well into the 1800s was based around the belief that the body had four humours or principal fluids. These were black bile, yellow bile, phlegm and blood, all of which needed to be in perfect balance if you were to remain in good health. To achieve that balance, bloodletting and enemas were needed, the former being administered via leeches and the latter through a greased tube attached to a pig's bladder.

The four humours were also linked with the four seasons: phlegm–winter, blood–spring, yellow bile–summer and black bile–autumn.

Obvious now you see it written down, isn't it?

With that kind of horrific quackery reigning supreme, it may well have been a mercy, albeit a small one, that childbirth in the Middle Ages wasn't seen as a medical happening.

The job of the medieval midwife was to ease the mother through childbirth with the tools she had at her disposal. These mainly consisted of stinking ointments, herbal salves and the odd magic gemstone.

When the baby was born, the midwife would bathe the child, rub them with salt and put honey around their tiny gums to stimulate their appetite. Then the infant would be wrapped in swaddling, like a well-seasoned joint of beef. Then, in perhaps the only part of the medieval birthing ritual that the occasional modern woman would pine for, the mother would remain in her lying-in chamber for a month, with only the midwife and her female pals permitted to see her and attend to her needs. As we will see, hundreds of years later the practice of lying in is still going strong in various parts of the world.

The beginning of the end of this age of stagnation and the reintegration of the knowledge and practices lost after the fall of Rome came thanks to Eucharius Rösslin, a German doctor who in 1513 wrote *Der Rosengarten* (*The Rose Garden*), which rapidly became a standard medical text for midwives. Drawing from his own observations and the wisdom of the ancients, specifically our old Greek friend Soranus, he began the transformation of birth. But not before he took an angry swipe at midwives, who he saw as ill-educated, shoddy charlatans who 'through neglect and oversight . . . destroy children far and wide'.

That isn't exactly a five star review, and together with the, albeit rudimentary, medicalisation of the process of labour, it puts us firmly on the road to the present day.

The two major changes that characterise a 'modern' birth as experienced by millions of women worldwide over the past century or so are that, while the ancient role of the midwife hasn't disappeared, it has an uneasy relationship with the (still) male dominated world of obstetric medicine at best – at worst, it has been relegated to very much a second-class status in the delivery room.

The second, even more profound, change revolves around where and how the delivery takes place.

The home birth and squatting delivery position have been replaced, with millions of women giving birth in hospitals while lying on their backs with their legs high in stirrups.

So how did these changes come about so quickly? How did centuries – millennia even – of practice and ritual get to be overturned so quickly?

As we've seen, the exclusive right to attend births had been held for centuries across swathes of the planet by midwives and female friends. In old English at least, these birthing pals were known as 'God sibs', meaning siblings in God. Over time, though, as the medical profession in particular and men in general began to frown on these all-female gatherings, the phrase 'God sibs' was heaped with negative connotation until its meaning shifted to mean a gathering of loose-lipped women – and the word we know today as gossip was born.[30]

The medicalisation of birth, which was started by the likes of medical men such as Rösslin, was later taken further by the advent of obstetric surgeons in seventeenth-century France, with François Mauriceau at the forefront of them all.

His 1668 publication *Traité des Maladies des Femmes Grosses et Accouchées* (*The Diseases of Women with Child*) almost singlehandedly established obstetrics as a distinct medical specialty and was translated into many languages.

This arrival of men of medicine into the hitherto exclusively female world of the birth gathered pace quickly. As well as bringing about a whole host of genuinely groundbreaking and life-saving advances, Mauriceau was also instrumental in precipitating another change that spread like wildfire and is only now beginning to be challenged, the horizontal delivery position.

As we've seen, for centuries women had been free to move around, squat, crouch and generally find the best approach to help them push out their baby.

Perhaps the most infamous tale in the entire history of birth is that of the French King Louis XIV. The story has it that, keen to get a better view of the birth of his child, the nosy monarch ordered his doctor to carry out the birth with the mother on her back.

It's impossible, of course, to be sure if that story is factually true, but what we do know is that Mauriceau held a prominent position in Louis' court and he was known to advocate that women lie down during birth in order to give the obstetric surgeon the best possible view and access to the business end of things – because, obviously, they were the most important people in the room!

Critics of this prone position point to the fact that as well as causing the weight of the uterus and the baby itself to put pressure on some pretty major blood vessels and the sciatica nerve during labour, it also reduces the pelvic opening by up to a third compared with vertical positions.

They also say that it's a position that asks a labouring mother to fight against gravity rather than using it to her advantage, and it is, in essence, more physician-friendly than patient-friendly.

While the last century has undoubtedly seen general birth survival rates increasing, it seems there is still a dichotomy at the heart of things. As we move on to the difference in birth practices today, it's worth noting that currently, as the debate rages in many industrialised countries about whether the medicalisation of birth, even with all the benefits it brings, has gone too far, 1 million babies still die each year across the planet within 24 hours of being born.[31]

Making the first day of a child's life the most dangerous by far.

Birth today

Before we look at how people currently give birth around the world, one point is worth making and worth making well.

Today, tomorrow and throughout the entirety of our history, human childbirth has been an excruciatingly, often terrifyingly and always uniquely painful experience.

The word 'uniquely' is used very deliberately, because the women of our species have for millennia been suffering at the hands of cephalopelvic disproportion, which despite being an explosion in a consonant factory, has a pretty simple and profound meaning – a human baby's head is very nearly too big to pass through the opening in its mother's pelvis.

Paging Mr Darwin.

It gets worse, though, because among our primate cousins there isn't a single one, not the bonobos, not the gibbons, not the cheeky chimps, who don't have much more room to spare when it comes to the baby–pelvis equation. Which means that our closest relatives pretty much push their young out in a matter of minutes while the females of our species are put through hour after hour of agony.

Why?

Firstly, having a big wide pelvis might well be a boon for popping out a baby, but it's not great if you have designs on being the smartest primate on the block by starting to walk on two feet. Walking upright, or bipedalism, was a huge step up our evolutionary ladder, but it came at a real cost – a set of evolutionary compromises like back pain and sore feet, which most of us still suffer from at some time or another, millions and millions of years after the extraordinary adaptation to become a bipedal species came about.

But the effect this drastic transformation had on the pelvis was by far the biggest anatomical change that happened over generations of natural selection – it fundamentally altered its shape, which meant that pushing a baby through it was significantly more difficult. Especially when, about 2 million years ago, the babies in question began to rapidly expand the size of their brains, which led to the situation women from hospital to hut, birthing pool to birthing stool find themselves in today – suffering huge pain and often life-threatening complications to push a baby that's too big through a hole that's too small.[32]

And so it is that birth remains a true ordeal for women everywhere today, and as such it's hardly surprising that so many practices, techniques and cultural idiosyncrasies still surround it. Delivering a baby is still a monumental undertaking that continues to take the lives of 800 women every single day, with 99% of those deaths occurring in the developing world.[33]

While that is still a shocking figure, it represents real progress – maternal mortality rates are believed to be falling by 1.4% each year.[34] One of the main factors behind that move is a shift in where and in what circumstances a huge percentage of the planet's babies are now born.

From home to hospital

The greatest single transformation in the post-war period in the realm of birth has been the acceleration of the move from home to hospital as the default place to undergo labour.

This trend had been gaining momentum throughout the twentieth century, but it's really in the last 25 years or so that it has all but totally replaced home births across huge parts of the planet.

The story of the UK's gradual shift to medicalised and institutionalised birth set a precedent which many other countries followed.

When lying-in hospitals started to be established in Britain in the mid-1700s, the creation of man-midwifery began, and it is estimated that within a generation or two a large proportion of all deliveries in England were attended by medical practitioners.[35] A medical revolution had started.

Not that it initially made much of a difference to maternal deaths, mind you. From 1850 to the mid-1930s the risk of a mother dying in childbirth remained stubbornly static.[36] It wasn't until the introduction of antibacterial drugs in 1936–37 that there was an incredibly steep decline in maternal deaths from puerperal fever, a bacterial infection contracted by women during childbirth or miscarriage.

Throughout this time the move from home to hospital had been gaining strength and by 1954 around 64% of deliveries took place in hospital. By 1972 that rate had moved to 91% and from 1975 onwards it has never dipped below 95% in the UK. This statistic shows no real signs of changing significantly any time soon, although there's been something of a resurgence in the popularity of home birthing, and despite the fact that NICE, the National Institute for Health and Care Excellence, recently said that hospital labour wards staffed by doctors should be for difficult cases only to avoid the danger of over-intervention.[37]

It's a very similar story across other industrialised nations too. In the United States, home births have declined from 50% in 1938 to account for less than 1% of all deliveries today, and in Japan it took just 25 years to move from 95% of all births taking place at home in 1950 to just 1.2% in 1975.[38]

Elsewhere, although the pattern of change may have been different, by and large the direction has been the same.

In China, for example, hospital births have almost completely replaced traditional home births except for the very poorest women or those in particularly remote areas. But experiences of hospital births can vary wildly depending on your social status, as is the case across much of the West too, of course. The wealthiest of urban Chinese women can give birth in luxurious private hospitals, while members of the emerging middle class tend to give birth at state-run hospitals with no choice of doctor and often in rooms with other women.

In Europe, the likes of Germany, France and Belgium, and even the normally 'other' Scandinavian countries, have seen home deliveries account for no more than 2% of all births for many years now.

But there is one country that has stemmed the rising tide of hospital rather than home births, almost singlehandedly in fact: the Netherlands.

The Dutch have 20% of their babies at home with a midwife in attendance – the highest rate in the Western world by some considerable distance. A recent survey carried out across the country also found that the risk of severe complications is one in 1,000 for home births and 2.3 in 1,000 for hospital births.[39] (The midwife is generally unable to administer pain relief medication. In fact, until very recently indeed, even in Dutch hospitals you only tended to get help if it fitted in with the anaesthetist's schedule rather than your birth plan, a phenomenon known locally as the 9–5 epidural.)

What's also interesting about the Netherlands is that when the OECD compiled data on perhaps the most indicative of all the medicalisation of birth indicators – the number of caesarean sections per 100 births – they came in with the smallest number of any developed or developing nation: 14.3%.[40]

Who do you think were the top four nations performing the most C-sections?

If Mexico, Turkey, China and Brazil were going to be your answer, congratulations. Although I don't believe you!

These four powerhouses of the new world economic order have taken to the caesarean route with a vengeance. In Brazil in particular the numbers are staggering, with 50% of all births being performed that way, a figure that rises above 80% for those with private health insurance.

While the home and natural birthing system clearly works for the Dutch, in truth they remain an anomaly. While movements for a return to home birthing and away from the clinical approach are gaining traction in the West, the figures always seem stubbornly entrenched when it comes to mothers who eventually find themselves in a hospital bed rather than their own.

It's tempting to decry this situation as another example of a world gone mad, science silencing sense, but that would be an oversimplification of a complex socio-political issue and would potentially ignore the harsh reality for millions of mothers worldwide.

Home births around the world

The notion of a planned home birth, supported by a trained midwife with a fully equipped and staffed modern medical facility within easy reach in a speedy ambulance, should never be compared with having a child at home for mothers who aren't lucky enough to be so well catered for.

On a trip to Tanzania I met a community down the coast from the capital Dar es Salaam who live on the vast network of deltas and mangrove swamps covering that area. For them, medical help is an estuary crossing away – and for most people that means a five-hour journey in a tiny wooden canoe across tidal waters to get to help. If you are heavily pregnant and experiencing complications you can either go by water or cut your way through the headland scrub in sheer desperation to reach a medical facility.

In Tibet, many woman still give birth at home either alone or with their husband or mother-in-law in attendance. Women who have just given birth are considered dirty or polluted and not only have to cut the umbilical cord themselves but do so using a knife that is cleaned afterwards rather than before its use to remove the pollution of childbirth. Many women also have to endure labour in an animal enclosure as a result of this belief about being unclean.

Unsurprisingly, with a start to life as harsh and dangerous as that, the infant mortality rate has been reported to be among the highest in the world, with 30% of Tibetan children failing to see their first birthday.[41]

These almost unimaginably horrific situations are what led to the 800 deaths from preventable causes related to pregnancy and childbirth every single day, with 99% of them occurring in developing countries where the medicalisation of birth and the move from home to hospital haven't taken place in anywhere near the numbers they have in countries further down the development line.

Finding a way to transform the ultra-clinical approach that the hospitalisation of birth has created, together with the loss of control and perceived lack of compassion, and to replace it with some of the values associated with more traditional practices is what the home or natural birth movement aspires to.

While the movement's success in terms of raw numbers may be slight, its impact on the way in which hospital births themselves are carried out is significant in countries with midwife-led units, which are becoming commonplace in the UK and even in China. These centres offer a halfway house between the strict medicalisation of the past 40 years in the West and a more holistic, predominantly female-led experience that takes its inspiration from generations gone by.

Leaving that aside, the fact remains that Save the Children's 2013 *State of the World's Mothers* report[42] listed the 10 worst places to become a mother as all being in sub-Saharan Africa and the top 10 exclusively made up of countries where birth is medicalised for the vast majority of mothers.

The hospital verses home birth debate remains as globally complex as it is emotive.

Myths and mantras of motherhood's earliest moments

The placenta

If the move towards hospital birth has left a line of discarded and debunked traditions in its wake, the way the mother and baby are treated afterwards couldn't be more different.

Modernity may have had its way with a handful of the more bizarre rituals but, on the whole, the arrival of a new life triggers a whole host of sacred and long-held beliefs and practices depending on where you are and which culture you hail from.

Before you've so much as thought about your baby, there is of course the placenta to deal with, or not depending on where you hail from.

For the untrained and perhaps uncultured eye like mine, a placenta merely resembled the inside of an alien's bagpipe – a mass of bloody and seemingly never ending membrane that I was very happy for the medical professionals to deal with in the appropriate sanitary manner.

And as for the umbilical cord – well, after severing it with surgical scissors (no one warns you how fibrous or altogether gristly it is), let's just say my relationship with sausages has never been quite the same since.

But it turns out that I am a philistine when it comes to these matters.

In many cultures, bringing a baby into the world isn't just a sacred event in itself, the leftovers are too, and simply disposing of them in a bio-waste bin is tantamount to begging for the worst of luck to befall the newborn and its mother.

In Cambodia, the mother's placenta is carefully wrapped in a banana tree leaf before being placed beside the newborn for three days so the baby can slowly get used to the separation before the placenta is then buried. While in India there's a tradition that sees the umbilical cord gently placed around the child's neck.

An often ornate box called a *kotobuki bako* is the home for the cord in traditional Japanese households. After being cleaned, it is placed inside as a keepsake and to help ensure a positive relationship between the mother and child.

That's not all, though. Many Japanese also keep part of their umbilical stump that drops off in early babyhood – and if they haven't got it, their mothers probably will have. Known as the *heso-no-o*, literally meaning 'tail of the belly', it is seen as something to be honoured and a vital link between mother and child.

Which is very lovely, even if we are talking about a piece of decades old dead flesh.

While the British have a pretty clinical approach to all things afterbirth, there was, for a short spell, a fad that saw people making placenta pâté to be eaten as a celebration of the new life.

In fact, a TV cookery show in the UK even featured a recipe being prepared and served at a birth party. The placenta was fried with shallots and garlic, flambéed, pureed and served on focaccia bread.

Mmmmm.

While the child's father had 17 helpings, the other guests were a whole lot less enthusiastic – but not, as it turned out, as unamused as the TV authorities who condemned the show as being offensive on the grounds of what else but taste.

Sitting the month

Afterbirth aside, once the delivery is safely over there seems to be a theme to the rituals, which occur across many countries and cultures. While they differ in detail they have much in common, despite apparently self-starting thousands of miles apart.

In India, for instance, most mothers follow some form of the traditional 40-day confinement and recuperation period after giving birth known in Hindi as the *Jaappa*. A special diet is followed to aid milk production, sex is forbidden and each day the new mum is given a massage to aid recovery.

Which all sounds lovely, but increasing work pressures and lack of family support because of relocation are seeing this ancient practice come under threat.

A very similar tradition exists across China, South Korea and Vietnam. 'Sitting the month' or 'doing the month' can see new mothers forbidden from bathing or showering for 30 days, presumably because contaminated water was once a common and potentially deadly threat.

Although far fewer new mums now adhere to this ancient wisdom, many are still expected to spend the first month resting indoors. They're usually looked after by their family, who take on the cooking and washing duties and generally keep the new mother away from any physical activity other than feasting on five warm meals a day, with copious bowls of chicken soup and other delicacies that are thought to stimulate the milk supply and restore health.

For those who can afford it, a new tradition has cropped up in China in recent years too – this sees families hire a *yue sao*, a qualified nursemaid who will also feed the baby at night. There are even special post-birth hotels you can check yourself into for a month or more if you don't think your relatives are up to helping out, and there are special catering companies that offer a three-meals-a-day home delivery service for new mothers.

It's a similar story in Japan: it is a cultural tradition that women stay in bed with their baby for 21 days. During this time friends may drop by to greet the new baby and join the family in eating the celebratory food *sekihan* (rice with red beans).

Once mother and baby are home, visitors flood in not only to give the baby a gift but also to receive one in return! Traditionally, it's something small, such as a bottle of perfume or candy, with a message from the baby attached to thank friends and family for the visit.

Who's a thoughtful bubba then!

Greece, too, has a traditional 40-day confinement called the *sarantisma*. At the end of the spell the baby is taken to the church for the first time and a special blessing made to draw the solitude to an end. Across Latin America we see a strikingly similar 40-day postpartum period called *la cuarentena* or the quarantine!

It's much nicer than it sounds, though.

Primarily facilitated by female relatives, rest is obligatory, wholesome plain food prepared and provided, and, as the new mother's body is considered open or vulnerable, she must cover her head and neck with garments and wrap her abdomen in a cloth called a *faja*.

Theories abound as to why this confinement tradition has occurred across continents and generations – a bolstering spell for the weak, new-born immune system, time and space for breastfeeding technique and routine to develop, or simply the need to develop the mother–child bond are all cited and credible.

In the case of the Latin American version, researchers even claim it originates from a passage in the Old Testament book of Leviticus that stipulates 40 days of purification after the birth of a son – and double for a daughter.

Whatever the origins of this multination ritual, one thing is for sure: the new mothers of most of northern Europe and North America have long since lost the chance to take it easy post-birth. The women who get nearest are those outliers of all things birth-related, the Dutch. As well as being the last refuge of the home birth, new mothers in the Netherlands enjoy the kind of state-provided post-birth care that most of the rest of the planet can only dream about.

Kraamzorg is available for everyone, whether they have a home or hospital birth, and involves a professional maternity nurse coming to the home and looking after both mother and baby for eight straight days.

The nurse shows the new mother how best to care for the baby and bathe them, and crucially helps mothers through the often difficult and painful first days of breastfeeding. Not only that, but if there are other children in the house, the nurse will help by looking after them too, making sure meals are prepared. They may also do a spot of laundry and light housekeeping.

I can ride a bike – can I be Dutch?

The Finnish baby box

North-east a touch, in Finland, there's another cool example of how new parents are given very practical help by the state.

And it all revolves around a cardboard box.

Since the 1930s, a maternity gift package has been given to all new-born children in Finland, no matter what background they're from, to ensure an equal start in life. The starter kit contains clothes, sheets, nappies and toys – and the box itself can even be used as the baby's first crib, a tradition that many Finns still keep to this day.

And for the parents there are even condoms. How very Scandinavian.

Mothers have a choice between taking the box or a cash grant, currently set at 140 euros, but 95% opt for the box, which has become a national institution. But initially this was much more than a mere gimmick – Finland was a poor nation in the 1930s with an infant mortality rate running at 65 deaths per 1,000 babies, but the figures improved rapidly in the decades that followed, thanks in part to the baby box.

The reason this smart, practical little gift (which was Finland's official present to the Duke and Duchess of Cambridge to celebrate the birth of their son George) is still going strong is because, no matter where you are in the world, no matter what language you speak, the first year of a child's life tests any parent to the absolute limit.

But while the challenges may remain the same wherever you find yourself, the ways in which different cultures deal with them often differ wildly – as we are about to see.

A parent's perspective

Kathy – UK, Germany and US

When I found out that I was expecting our first, we were in the UK, had no experience of pregnancy, or of babies, so had no idea of what to expect during pregnancy or the birth.

I saw the GP once during my pregnancy; the rest of the prenatal checks were all with a midwife. I wasn't given a list of things I couldn't eat or do – I was told to carry on as usual. We were encouraged to go to antenatal classes, where I remember most of the talk centring around the birthing process and what pain relief would be on offer. There wasn't a great choice: the central London hospital we went to offered gas and air or an epidural. We could always hire a TENS machine from Boots beforehand and start getting used to that, as it would be very helpful in the first stages of labour, we were told.

It wasn't.

During the labour the gas and air had made me throw up so the only other choice to help me deal with my son's 42cm head was to take the epidural. I was petrified of the things and tried to quiz the anaesthetist about the risks of me being paralysed. He was quite reassuring, but unluckily for me I turned out to be one of the few who had something go wrong. Once the pain relief kicked in, my body was perfectly divided through my belly button into one wonderfully pain-free half and one half that was still in agony. As I had one of the self-controlling epidurals I was told to try topping myself up a couple of times. By the time they realised I wasn't making it up, the anaesthetist was called and he had to give me a second shot. After that, I couldn't feel anything from the waist down and had to be told from the monitor when the contractions were happening and when to push.

Ben was finally born at 10.01, and after the lovely midwife had checked I was registered to a GP's surgery, they had me patched up and ready to leave by 1p.m. – albeit in a wheelchair as my legs were still paralysed.

My second and third children were born in Germany. One in a large, ultra-modern birthing unit of the town hospital and one in a local cottage hospital where I was the only labour they had had all week.

The German approach is to put you under the care of an OB/GYN [obstetrics/gynaecology] doctor for the entirety of the pregnancy, and if you wish you get some midwife visits afterwards, although it is up to you to select one, like you would a babysitter.

I decided to have an 'ambulant' birth, meaning I wanted to leave straight away afterwards. Not many people do that in Germany, possibly because the hospitals are really comfortable and the food is really good. Pain relief was never really discussed with me, and I only found out by chance through my midwife that if I wanted an epidural I would have to go along to the hospital a week or so before the birth to have a blood test.

When it actually came round to the birth of my second, I was examined by the doctor at the hospital then left in a room to have a really uncomfortable ECG of the baby. I had to lie still on my back, which I always find really uncomfortable in labour. When I threw up and asked to move, I was told I had hours to go and that I had to stay there a bit longer. I got quite stroppy by this point and said it was really painful and I had to move around. When the nurse eventually believed me and let me start moving around, she examined me and then said sorry, I was too far along and that I would have to stop pacing and it was too late for any pain relief. She then broke my waters, which hadn't happened, without asking me, and then my son was born very quickly. He didn't cry and seemed to be in shock, so the doctors said I couldn't go home.

The third birth was similar, but I had the whole staff running round after me. They let me stay in the birthing bath until right at the end, which wasn't very long, and then, strangely enough, it was too late for any pain relief as well. I don't know anyone in Germany who didn't have a caesarean section who actually got to hospital in time to have pain relief. Having said that, though, I felt great after each birth and could have gone back to work the next day, unlike after my first one. I did feel though that I wasn't the important one in the process – it was all very focused on the baby.

My fourth baby was born in New York State. The experience was very different, primarily I'm sure because at this point in our lives we had very good health insurance and some people aren't so lucky. You are also under the care of an OB/GYN in the US, but they do take the whole business a lot more seriously. I do remember my doctor telling me that I had left it too late and that I should have consulted her before the pregnancy if I wanted to have a girl this time. There are, I was told, 'things' you can do or diets you can follow if you want to influence gender.

When I was in labour I was offered a lot of pain relief. When I said I'd be OK, I was told to think long and hard about it as the anaesthetist would have to go into surgery in a few minutes and then he would have been unavailable for several hours. The nurses came in all the time with a pain ladder, to ask me constantly on a scale of one to 10 what level was my pain at. I felt like I let them down when I kept saying it was manageable. We were just busy trying to watch all the films we could before the baby came out.

When my daughter (I must have unwittingly been eating the right things!) was born, she was taken away from me so that I could get some rest and she could be checked over. I hadn't fed her or anything, and after a few long hours I got quite stressed. I think I was supposed to be enjoying the peace, but it felt very weird to me.

She was brought back to me eventually, but they did ask me if I wanted to have her taken care of in the nursery overnight, or if I wanted her brought back to me just for feeding, or if I wanted her all night alone. They asked me this every night I was in there, and I think I stayed three nights in total. The high point was definitely the dinner on night two, for both my husband and me, with sparkling (alcohol-free) grape juice to wash it down. I had lobster and my husband had steak. It was like being in a hotel, where you were the guest of honour. Although a hotel where you weren't allowed to walk around holding your baby – all babies had to be in wheeled cots if you were going anywhere.

I loved the whole experience, but I'm not sure who wouldn't. The whole process was designed to make the mother feel as relaxed as possible, but it was one that came with a hefty price tag, costing the health insurance $30,000.

WORLDLY WISDOM - PREGNANCY AND BIRTH

The length of a human pregnancy is calculated the same way everywhere on the planet at 40 weeks long.

Everywhere that is except France, where it's 41 weeks.

A host of international studies have found that stress during pregnancy in particular has been linked to a shorter gestation and a higher incidence of preterm birth, an increased risk of miscarriage and problems with attention and emotional reactivity in the child's later life.

Delivering a baby is still a monumental undertaking that continues to take the lives of 800 women every single day across the planet. Of those, 90% occur in the developing world.

The British government announced that from April 2015 both parents will be able to share 12 months of leave after the birth of a child. The move was heralded as groundbreaking, which it generally is, except that in Sweden they have enjoyed the right since 1974.

Paid parental leave has been available for many years in most countries – with the only exceptions being Papua New Guinea, Swaziland, Lesotho, Liberia and the United States of America.

In the UK in 1954, around 64% of deliveries took place in hospital. By 1972 that rate had moved to 91% and from 1975 onwards it has never dipped below 95%, a trend that has been replicated across almost all of the industrialised world – except, that is, for the Netherlands, which sees one in five babies born at home.

3
Looking after baby

The first year
Global game plans for the biggest job of your life

No matter where you call home, no matter what culture has shaped you and no matter how much advice from old wives, new doctors or indeed books like this very one you may have gleaned, the first few years of parenthood are a journey the like of which you'll never experience again.

It all really begins when the immediate post-birth interest and buzz – in whatever way that manifests itself where you are – has begun to die down and you are first left alone with a small, warm bundle who relies on you for its very survival.

That momentous fact tends to focus the mind somewhat, which is a good thing because there's a lot to learn and adapt to and a whole load of sleep to miss out on while you're doing it.

But before we look at who does what where when it comes to bringing up baby, we need a name and we need it fast.

The name game

Leaving aside the breast versus bottle debate, which we will look at together with all sorts of other food-related issues later on, one of the first major tasks that befalls parents across the globe is bestowing a name on their child – and the timing, technique and traditions around doing so are diverse and fascinating.

The majority of parents these days seem to want a name for their child that will perform two diametrically opposed functions.

Firstly it needs to avoid being too common. Being one of five people in class to answer to the same name is not cool. We are all individuals; we all need our own space and identity.

Secondly it needs to avoid being too uncommon. Being the only person in your school with a weird name is not cool. We are social animals and we all need to feel like we belong.

Things haven't always been this way, though.

To be born in Elizabethan England, for instance, was to be named after one of your godparents. Not just any old godparent, mind you – one carefully chosen by your parents for their financial status or high social stature. The aim was for you to be the apple of their eye and to benefit financially thanks to the ultimate act of tribute – taking their name.

This had the effect – along with there being no mass media, of course – of making the pool of names people were choosing from considerably smaller than it is today. The number of acceptable names during this time was significantly smaller than what's on offer today, with Elizabeth, Anne, Joan, Margaret, Alice, Mary and Agnes accounting for around 65% of all girls' names and John, Thomas, William, Richard and Robert doing likewise for the boys.

It won't surprise you to hear that the Puritans of the *Mayflower* age liked a biblical name or two for their children. They even added some virtuous ones like Charity, Joy, Mercy, Grace, Prudence and Hope into the lexicon, which still thrive today. What didn't take off in quite the same way were the slightly more extreme examples. 'Fear-God', for instance, hasn't become a huge hit, and nor has 'Jesus-Christ-came-into-the-world-to-save'. Quite why 'No-merit' or 'Sin-deny' didn't gain worldwide traction is a mystery though, and 'If-Christ-had-not-died-for-thee-thou-hadst-been-damned' must surely make a comeback one day in the naming charts.

Another remnant from a bygone age are the various naming ceremony traditions that take place around the world. In China you could find yourself invited to a 'Red Egg and Ginger' baby-naming party – a celebration held after the baby's first month of life. The egg, considered a delicacy in ancient China, represents fertility and is dyed red for good luck. Waiting four weeks to officially name the baby is significant and also fuels a widespread Chinese superstition, also seen in Vietnam, that views naming a child any earlier as asking for the most awful bad luck to befall it. What lies behind this one-month delay are the high infant mortality rates of the past. Scores of babies never made it to a month and so to name them before that milestone had been reached was considered foolhardy.

This led to the phenomenon of the fake or 'milk' name. Designed to trick evil spirits into staying away from the child, the most undesirable terms imaginable were given to these beautiful newborns in the hope that disgusted spirits would move on to the next family. So from Ugly and Rat to Mud Face and Excrement, all sorts of not-so-cute nicknames were used!

Once that little spell has been broken, though, and it comes to choosing the real name, the Chinese believe that each child is unique and should carry an individual moniker. With thousands of characters in their alphabet, this is more possible than it would be in most other languages. But even with so many to choose from, when you are the planet's most populous nation, it's inevitable that words like *Mei*, meaning beautiful, are popular for girls.

A more modern-day Chinese phenomenon, and one I have to admit (if a little shamefacedly) I was very grateful for when I visited, was the increasingly popular practice of choosing a Western name in early adulthood. When fiscal reforms brought foreign investment and foreign visitors, this trend soon took hold as people no doubt became sick of people like me butchering their traditional Chinese names in an attempt to pronounce them. Some go for traditional titles, while others choose words for their meanings – for instance, an Oak I know in China is very much the strong and sturdy character he chose to be named after.

More still look toward popular culture for inspiration – I met both a Rambo and a Hugh (Grant) on my travels.

And China isn't the only country where culture and language meld to form a new naming regime. In Costa Rica, for example, as Spanish and English increasingly wash up against each other, English names are being taken but are spelled how they sound in Spanish to create Spanglish names such as Mery for Mary and Maykol for Michael.

Elsewhere, systems have long been employed to help out with naming duties. In parts of India, for example, the first male child is named after the paternal grandfather and the second male child after the maternal grandfather, with the girls being named after their paternal and maternal grandmothers. If you are from southern India, where a father's name is often used as a surname too, you can have quite a confusing time on your hands.

In Nigeria, babies from the Yoruba community are initially given an *oruko* name based on the circumstances of their birth. So Abegunde, for example, is for a boy born during a holiday, while a girl born during a rainy spell may be called Bejide, which means just that. Further down the line the children are also given an *oriki* or praise name that expresses wishes for their future – Titilayo is 'eternal happiness', for instance – or even hopes that the parents hold, like the poignant Dunsimi, which, in a part of the world where infant mortality rates are still relatively high, translates as 'don't die before me'.

Many Polish names derive from those of Christian saints and it is quite common for people to celebrate their saint's day in much the same way they do for their birthday, so much so that places displaying the date, like billboards and buses, also flash the names of that day's particular patron saints.

But perhaps it's beautiful Bali where you'll find the most strict of all the naming formulas. Balinese children are named according to birth order, with firstborns being able to choose from Wayan, Putu, Gede or Nengah, second-borns being called Made or Kadek, the third in line taking their pick from either Nyoman or Komang, and the fourth being called Ketut – whether they like it or not.

Have a fifth child and the whole thing goes round again!

Which would be confusing enough were it not for the fact that all of those names are used for both boys and girls and that the Balinese often use only one name, so there isn't even a surname or family name to use for reference. Nicknames abound as a result, of course, but when it comes to official documents things can get very tricky indeed.

On the other side of the coin, many parts of the world have seen almost anything go when it comes to what people call their kids. Often led by celebrity culture and mass media, all sorts of weird and wonderful titles come to light – but there is something of a regulatory fightback under way.

Germany, Sweden, China, Denmark, France, Spain, Argentina and Japan all restrict the names that parents can use in one way or another, and in Iceland the authorities insist on certain grammatical rules being met, gender lines respected and the child saved from any possible future embarrassment. To ensure that happens, there's an official list of 1,853 female names and 1,712 male ones for parents to choose from, or they have to seek permission from a special committee if they want to go off-piste.

In Germany, when a couple wanted to call their baby Osama Bin Laden the state intervened on the basis of child welfare. The decision making isn't always so clear-cut, though. In New Zealand, for instance, the authorities refused the name Yeah Detroit, but allowed Number 16 Bus Shelter! In the US, where almost anything goes, there have been babies called Enamel, Lettuce, Mutton and Post Office. Though not all in the same family.

But beyond all the tradition versus celebrity wayoutness and among all the annual league tables now published about our naming habits, are names still important in a world awash with Twitter, Facebook and Weibo handles?

By way of an answer let me tell you a little something about myself.

I like to think that as I rapidly approach my fortieth year I'm mellowing somewhat.

Not that I've ever really been a huge hothead, you understand, but those odd things that used to get my goat in the flush of youth aren't seeming so important now somehow.

Maybe it's the lack of energy now I've got young children to keep me on my toes, who knows? But whatever the reason, total and utter failure to indicate at a junction by fellow drivers, for instance, is now met with a shrug of the shoulders rather than the steaming of the ears.

But I've noticed one little quirk that doesn't seem to be following the same pattern, and that seems to be pressing more and more buttons as I get older – and it's only a single letter.

You wouldn't think the difference between Wood and Woods had the potential to be a major goat getter, but for some reason the missing off of that little 's' I find impossible to ignore.

It's only a name though, right? It doesn't really matter, does it?

Well, in fact, there's mounting evidence to suggest that our names carry much more meaning, weight and lifelong significance than we might imagine. It's beginning to look like the ancient Roman expression *nomen est omen*, or name is destiny, has more to it than meets the eye as scientific studies have shown that the world makes assumptions based on names on a range of areas including our ethnicity, social background and even academic potential.

A test carried out in the United States demonstrated that teachers, being as human as the rest of us, are more than capable of marking work based on the perceptions conjured up by a particular name rather than the merits of what's in front of them. A group of 80 very experienced teachers were each given four essays, all of similar quality, and asked to mark them. The only identification on them was a first name and a false last initial. The names used were two traditional ones, David and Michael, and two more unusual examples, Elmer and Hubert.

Before starting their experiment, the researchers predicted that the essays 'written' by the children with common, popular names would be graded higher – and their prediction proved to be absolutely correct. The Davids were given the highest marks, closely followed by the Michaels and with Elmer trailing in third, and Hubert – poor, unusually named Hubert – was marked well and truly bottom of the pile.

To ensure that this finding was accurate, the same papers with the same names were given to 80 undergraduates in the relevant field to grade, and the result was interesting. No discernible pattern at all could be detected in who got what marks. The teachers, it seemed, had developed positive attitudes towards children with more popular names and a corresponding negative one towards those with the more standout ones.[43]

Very similar findings came out of an anonymous survey of 2,000 German primary school teachers. If you're a Charlotte, Sophie, Marie, Hannah, Alexander, Maximilian, Simon, Luke or Jacob, you get a gold star just for making it out of kindergarten. But happen to be called Chantal, Mandy, Angelina, Justin, Maurice or Kevin – especially Kevin – and your teacher won't be at all surprised if you turn out to have a behavioural disorder.[44]

Hop over to the UK and it's the same, with more than one in three teachers who responded to a sizable survey saying they 'expected' Aliesha, Casey, Crystal, Kyle, Liam and Brooklyn to be a handful in class and Elizabeth, Charlotte and Emma to be well-behaved young ladies! What's more, half of the teachers polled admitted that they make these assumptions when they take their first look at the register at the start of the school year.[45]

Then there's nominative determinism, the concept that our names play a part in the jobs or professions that we end up doing. Would Usain Bolt be as fast if he was called Usain Meander?

And Edmund Akenhead was surely born to be the crossword editor of *The Times* – a position he did indeed hold from 1965 to 1983.

Could Belgian footballer Mark De Man really have done anything else with his life, and should we be surprised when we discover that Buzz Aldrin's mother's maiden name was Marion Moon?

Perhaps one of the starkest studies carried out in the field of names was the 'Are Emily and Greg more employable than Lakisha and Jamal?' paper, where almost 5,000 fake CVs were sent out in response to job advertisements in Chicago and Boston newspapers. Half of the résumés were given names that sounded like they belonged to white people – Emily Walsh or Greg Baker, for example – and the other half were given names that sounded African American, like Lakisha Washington or Jamal Jones.

The results were conclusive and depressing.

The call-back rate from employers was 50% higher for the 'white' names than the 'black' names. The researchers inferred, and it's not hard to see why, that employers were using first names to discriminate unfairly against black candidates, perhaps at an unconscious level. Perhaps not.

Snobbery, social science or reinforcement of existing prejudices? Whatever's behind it, there's enough evidence in both the naming rituals that have built up around the planet and the research into impacts of what we are called to suggest that, as parental decisions go, choosing a name is right up there in terms of importance.

What I do know for sure is that one moment in my own life brought home just how important names are to us as individuals. Our youngest son was born at 34 weeks, way before my wife and I had settled on a name.

As the 4.5lb little mite lay in his incubator in the special care baby unit of a south London hospital, a card on the side read simply, all too simply, Baby Woods.

Not having a name seemed to make him all the more vulnerable. In a certain sense he needed to be called something to show that he was there, a little person in his own right fighting to live.

He did make it and he's called Louis. Louis Woods. With an 's'.

Is nurture natured or nurtured?

Whatever the name, on the face of it a baby is a baby is a baby. Right?

Regardless of where they happen to be born, these tiny powerhouses are no respecters of circumstance or experience and demand attention, unfailing love and a work ethic of quite frightening proportions from the people who brought them forth.

Likewise, there can't possibly be anything more universal across our entire species than the maternal instinct? The compelling urge to protect and nurture one's children is surely the most basic characteristic shared by even the most diversely different societies around the world.

All of which is true and was confirmed in part by a study carried out by the US-based Eunice Kennedy Shriver National Institute of Child Health and Human Development, which compared maternal behaviour in Argentina, Belgium, Brazil, France, Israel, Italy, Japan, Kenya and the United States and collated observations and data when babies reached five months old.[46]

Regardless of culture, mothers were found to feed, wash, change, talk to, play with and give toys to their babies. In fact, no matter which country they were in, apart from those six key behaviours, no other action of any statistical significance was noted as occurring regularly between mother and child. They were seen to be the fundamentals when it came to motherhood absolutely everywhere.

Another commonality found by the study was that, when carrying out these tasks, all mothers across the nine countries did so in two distinct ways: dyadic behaviour, where the mother was involved in social exchanges with the baby, like looking, talking, smiling and social play; and extradyadic behaviour, where the mother also encouraged her baby to pay attention to play materials, sounds, sights or other people besides herself.

When you take a moment to consider just how diverse a line-up of nations Argentina, Belgium, Brazil, France, Israel, Italy, Japan, Kenya and the United States are, those similarities are quite something and represent a testament not only to the universality of motherhood but to its single-minded intensity too.

But, of course, although the core fundamentals of nurturing a baby in its first year of life may be essentially the same across the geographical board, the way in which environment and circumstance shape the psychology and cultural belief systems of parents often creates huge differences of approach and technique. Often what one culture perceives as normal and utterly desirable for a child of a particular age can garner nothing short of horror and revulsion from another.

As we will soon see in greater detail, the complicated and fractious world of sleep is a prime example of this. While many in Western Europe and North America think nothing of getting a baby into a bedtime routine by letting them cry themselves out, many other countries around the world are shocked at the very notion of somehow 'teaching' a baby to sleep, let alone leaving it in distress as part of doing so.

To vast swathes of those on Planet Parent, consciously allowing a baby to cry, even for a moment, is considered cruel and unnatural. Yet elsewhere there are detailed guidebooks published and purchased in big numbers on how to do just that in the most effective and efficient way possible.

I had my own moment of cultural crossover when talking to a roomful of expectant couples in Beijing. Up on stage before me was a very traditional Chinese midwife who demonstrated (on a doll, thankfully) a nappy-changing technique so vigorous and brusque that it made my eyes water. With China having negotiated 1.35 billion successful births, I didn't think it my place to question this woman's approach in case it was a long-held and much-loved national way of doing things.

As it turned out, it wasn't – most of the expectant parents were slack-jawed at the way the doll was tossed around like pizza dough too.

Likewise, as someone from the UK, when I see – as I'm often privileged enough to do – many mothers in East Africa carrying their babies on their backs as they go about their day, I not only look on in awe but also acknowledge that whatever perceived childcare wisdom you may carry with you is just that – perceived – interpreted by you and based mainly on where and by whom you yourself were raised and what your particular cultural norms are.

In the case of the babies of Kenya and Tanzania, the *kanga* garment used to wrap nippers close onto their mothers' backs has the effect, in my experience, of creating youngsters so content and beautifully peaceful that you wonder why the rest of the world didn't adopt them long ago too. Perhaps we shared them once but dropped them in favour of enormous metal prams that are impossible to get on and off a bus without the help of at least three adults.

And so it is with the research mentioned earlier. Although the general principles and patterns of behaviour seem to be universal between a mother and her new child, how those behaviours manifest themselves can vary in subtle but hugely significant ways. Beneath the broad truths that the research found, it also discovered a clutch of variations. Babies in Italy and Argentina are spoken to much more often than they are in Belgium. In terms of social interaction with their babies, the same pattern is found: Argentine mothers come top again with Belgian mothers once again the most restrained. Out of the list, American mothers are most likely to give toys to their babies and actively encourage sitting alone, rolling over and crawling.

Is it reading too much into things to deduct that American mothers, steeped in a culture that puts individual freedom above all else, are most likely to encourage their babies to get on the move from an early age, and even to reward them for doing so with toys? The study's creators didn't think so and surmised that their findings supported the view that mothers make decisions about the way they interact with their babies based on different cultural cues that they may not even be aware of.

Another study reinforced this view. It found that, whereas middle-class US mothers were keen to maximise their child's cognitive development by providing 'stimulation', to Italian mothers the very word 'stimulation' in the context of their children meant something very different – to them it was primarily given to develop their social rather than purely cerebral abilities. That clear prioritisation of emotional intelligence over traditional cognition could be seen as establishing a very different blueprint for what is truly important in life from day one.[47]

On perhaps a more practical, less psychological day-to-day level at the parenting coalface, teething, as universal an early parental problem as you can imagine, throws up a typically broad range of approaches that have evolved in different parts of the world.

The Germans, for instance, call on crisp crunchy toast – *Zwieback*, meaning baked twice – as a teething biscuit, with biscotti being Italy's version. According to India's Ayurvedic tradition, cloves are useful for reducing inflammation and soothing sore gums. Ground cloves can be made into simple paste by adding water and, with a clean finger, a small portion is gently massaged into the gum. Anyone who has ever applied clove oil to an aching tooth knows this remedy works – but essentially numbs the entire mouth to do so!

Amber, with its anti-inflammatory and therapeutic properties, is recognised by many naturopathic health practitioners as a natural analgesic for relieving pain, including the pain of teething. Its secret ingredient is succinic acid, a compound released by the amber resin and absorbed by the body when the stone is worn next to warm skin. Amber from the Baltic region of Estonia, Latvia and Lithuania is thought to be especially rich in this healing substance. Teething necklaces made from amber have been used for centuries in the Baltic and elsewhere where natural amber is found.

Then, of course, there's Sophie, the all-conquering giraffe! First produced in France in 1961, its chewy, cold rubber and eminently biteable little snout has made it a global smash hit when it comes to toys to dribble over, with more of them sold in its native France each year than there are babies born.

Homeopathic granules have long been part of the teething technique in the UK. These come in small sachets that you pour into your toddler's mouth. As ever with homeopathic remedies, outside the anecdotal testimonies of those who swear by them, there's next to no proof the granules work beyond giving the child something else to think about for a minute or so. A clue to their longevity may lie in the fact that they often contain sugar, which, as we all know, works wonders on the distraction front, but not so much in the dental care direction.

There's even a remedy originally from Africa that still occasionally makes an appearance in the Caribbean and United States and that relies purely on the powers of the humble egg. When signs of teething are first detected, mothers place a raw egg upright in a sock or bag and tie it above where their baby sleeps and then wait for the magic of the yolky goodness to do the rest.

It may sound very unlikely, but at 4.18a.m. you'll try just about anything that's to hand or has been passed down via your oral parenting tradition.

Teeny tiny teeth aside, the very notion of childcare itself differs from place to place too. While the norm across much of the planet revolves around parents looking after their own offspring in a very linear fashion, in many cultures the care of children is often shared by the greater community and it is expected that children will not be raised exclusively by their parents.

For example, children raised in rural, semi-nomadic homes in the Sahara are often raised by groups of mothers and sisters in the community. These female networks support each other in providing food and childcare. Some Côte d'Ivoire villages see every member visit each newborn as soon as possible after birth to encourage relationships between the child and members of the community. And in Bali, mothers carry their babies in slings and are able to hand them over to nearby villagers whenever they need help.

This community approach can seem eminently sensible and even highly desirable, unless you live in an urban environment where your next-door neighbour of many years remains an almost complete stranger to you.[48]

But there are also cultures that haven't just developed different approaches to the early challenges of childcare, their view of very young children is utterly unique too.

The Beng, a small ethnic group in West Africa, assume that very young children are born as supremely spiritual beings and know and understand everything that is said to them, in whatever language they are addressed.

Parents believe in a spirit world where children live before birth and where they know all human languages and understand all cultures. Because life in the spirit world is very pleasant, children are often very reluctant to leave it for an earthly family. When they are born, they remain in contact with this other world for several years, and may decide to return there if they are not properly looked after.

So parents treat young children with care so that they're not tempted to return, and also with reverence, because these babies remain in contact with the spirit world.

You can surmise how this elaborate and quite beautiful and unique model came about – cripplingly high infant mortality rates were the catalyst for a cultural mechanic that encouraged parents to look after young children especially well. It was constructed to serve an important parental purpose, and although it could be looked on quizzically by those from different cultures, the Beng and their rather wonderful concept of spiritual, all-knowing children are just another ingenious way in which Planet Parent has evolved to cope with the diverse challenges often faced in protecting and nurturing very young children.

But if ever there was a perfect example of how adversity and environmental challenges created something truly magnificent in the realms of parenting, it's the amazing story of kangaroo care.

This now widespread technique based on skin-to-skin contact between a parent and their preterm baby sees tiny babies wearing only nappies and held in an upright position against the parent's bare chest – similar to the way a joey clings to its mother – for multiple periods throughout the day.

The method was dreamt up in 1978 by Colombian paediatrician Edgar Rey in response to woefully inadequate and limited incubator care in the Bogotá hospital where he worked. In desperation, he began to tuck infants into the gowns of their mothers in lieu of any other way of helping them.

The positive results were instant and astonishing, and from those humble beginnings kangaroo care has blossomed to become a modern miracle of early childcare – albeit one based on ancient principles.

Research has made it clear that the method is more than just an alternative to incubator care because it has proved to be an effective way to maintain body temperature and to stimulate breastfeeding and bonding, irrespective of setting, weight, gestational age and clinical conditions.

As well as increased parent–infant bonding, it's thought the baby also gains great comfort from hearing the parent's heartbeat and even increases their oxygen levels too.

This inspiring success story has now spread way beyond South America – my premature son, many, many miles away in south London, benefited from it. As well as helping him, the fact that I could do something proactive and positive during a time when feelings of utter helplessness abounded was a highly welcome side effect.

The method has been such a hit that it is now being used on full-term babies as well and achieving similar results. In fact, the only fly in the ointment is that in developed countries it's not being used enough due to ready access to incubators and technology and the assumption that they represent the best form of treatment.

The doctor from Bogotá knew different, though!

Sleep
Do parents everywhere feel this knackered?

I n the days before becoming a parent, you don't really appreciate sleep.

I mean you enjoyed it, luxuriated in it and occasionally overindulged in it on those days when getting out of bed was something other people did. But you don't really know or understand just how much you'll miss it once you become entirely responsible for the survival, upkeep and all-round development of another human being.

Who wakes up really early.

If you were fully aware of that fact, you would, in your pre-parent days, take weeks off work to do nothing but sloth – or, as I did on a rare lie-in opportunity recently, set the alarm just so you can experience the blissful moment when you turn it off, turn over and turn back in for hours' more kip.

I realise that sounds odd, obsessive even, but, as we are about to discover, sleep is a powerful drug and entire movements have sprung up, especially in Europe and North America these past decades, to try to help babies see sense when they insist on interrupting their parents' night of much-needed kip. The thing is, though, research has shown that not that long ago we all, regardless of our age or location, would have slept in shorter bursts.

So are babies just doing what comes naturally and is it us adults, especially in the West, who are getting out of bed the wrong side and harbouring unrealistically high expectations of a good night's sleep?

Let's find out.

The story of sleep

Everyone sleeps. We all need it and not getting enough of it can take a hefty toll on us physically and psychologically. In fact, the withholding of sleep has been used to devastating effect as a torture technique by many of the world's regimes to break subjects down and extract information. As well as the change in the psychological state that too little sleep can bring about, it also affects the body's immune system and hits neurobiological functions, with reaction time, memory and cognitive performance all going very soft, very quickly.

If you really start to lack sleep, hallucinations will quickly follow, bringing a sense of altered reality that is actually caused by the dreamy state of rapid eye movement activity beginning to force its way into wakefulness and creating a whole new nightmarish level of daydream.

Keep that woeful set of circumstances up for any length of time and your emotional state will begin to seriously degrade, swiftly followed by your moral compass spinning around like a lawn sprinkler before psychosis well and truly sets in.

Yes, sleep really *is* important.

Perceived wisdom says that we all need a good eight hours' sleep a day. But, as with an awful lot of those general dictates, this just doesn't hold true for many. Of course, we don't all need the same amount of sleep to be able to function well – history seems to be littered with people who have achieved much on very little shut-eye indeed. Perhaps the two most famous British prime ministers of all time – Winston Churchill and Margaret Thatcher – were both notoriously short sleepers, as were Napoleon and Florence Nightingale. Thomas Edison, it's said, regarded sleep as a dreadful waste of time and preferred to take short naps rather than a single long stretch.

As it happens, there's increasing evidence to suggest that the American inventor was onto something – although, ironically, his work could well have played a major role in changing sleep for the worse forever.

You see, thanks to his invention of the electric light bulb and subsequent widespread availability of artificial light, sleep patterns in the industrialised world have shifted significantly. A matter of a few hundred years ago, the time when your baby slept in the evening and the time you slept would have been much closer together simply because, once it was dark, people generally soon went to bed and then rose again at dawn.

Crucially, though, this didn't mean that people had an unbroken sleep from dusk until dawn, thus racking up many more hours than we manage these days. Rather, up until Edison *et al.* had their light bulb moments, we all slept in more segmented spells – as much of the animal kingdom still does today.

Yes, I'm looking at you cats.

It has been suggested that this split sleeping pattern was made up of a block from shortly after dark until midnight, followed by two hours awake for food (and sex), before it was back down for another three or four hours ahead of the sun coming up on a new day.[49]

Sounds nice, doesn't it?

In the few nomadic or hunter-gatherer societies that still exist today, this split sleeping has survived. It's the rest of us who have taken to expecting to 'sleep through', and, by extension, to want the same from our children. When put into this historical context, this seems all the more unfair an ask.

But even among the vast swathes of the industrialised world, significant differences exist in how we sleep. A major study of 10 countries in 2005 revealed that, while the global average time slept by the study participants was about 7.5 hours a night, the results from individual countries varied from 6 hours 53 minutes in Japan to 8 hours 24 minutes in Portugal.

Over 42% of Brazilians took regular afternoon naps, while only 12% of Japanese had a daytime doze. Over 32% of Belgians complained of insomnia and other sleep problems, while nearby neighbours Austria saw only 10% of people say the same.

In South Africa, 53% of respondents admitted they regularly used sleep medications, as did 46% of the Portuguese, which perhaps explains why they get such a luxuriant night's sleep.[50]

Another study, carried out by the OECD in 2009, indicated that the average French person sleeps almost 9 hours a night, closely followed by Americans and Spaniards (with 8.5 hours), while the Koreans and Japanese languish at the bottom of the list with substantially less than 8 hours.[51]

So we've established that adults vary based on nationality in terms of sleep, but what about children? A study of almost 30,000 families across the globe found that sleep among infants and toddlers, including naps, varied from 13.3 hours in New Zealand and 12.9 hours in the United States down to just 11.6 hours in Japan (as you may have already picked up, by all accounts the Japanese are the most sleep-deprived people on the planet). And average bedtimes for babies ranged from about 7.30p.m. in New Zealand to 10.45p.m. in Hong Kong.[52]

Does it really matter, though, if babies get a few hours less sleep a day here than they do there? It'll all come out in the wash anyway, won't it? By the time they are teenagers, won't we all need dynamite to get them up and out of bed, no matter where we are? Other than being exhausting for parents, having a baby who doesn't sleep all that well can't do any long-term harm, can it?

Dr Elsie Taveras, chief of general paediatrics at Massachusetts General Hospital for Children, has discovered that it can.

Together with her colleagues, she followed babies every year from six months until they were seven years old and at each visit recorded height, weight, body fat, waist and hip circumference as well as sleep habit information.

What her team found was that, even by seven, children with the worst sleep patterns throughout their young lives so far had the highest rates of obesity and body fat, especially abdominal fat, which is believed to be associated with heart disease and diabetes. The findings were clear: consistently disrupted sleep throughout childhood can have a cumulative, long-term and hugely detrimental effect on health.[53]

No pressure then.

So we know it matters and we also know – thanks to perhaps the most bizarre experiment ever devised by one of the world's most respected seats of learning – that a baby's cry is specifically designed not just to rouse us but also to make us react super-quickly.

To unearth this, Oxford University researchers had volunteers play the hammer-based arcade game 'Whack-A-Mole' after listening to babies crying, then again after sounds of adults in distress, and for a third time having heard birdsong with a similar sound profile to the cries of an infant.

Guess what? The participants' scores were higher after listening to the sound of crying babies.

Much higher.

For both the men and women in the study, their ability to react at speed and whack those pesky moles was significantly sharper than after the other two sounds. Anyone who has ever heard a baby cry knows that it has a unique ability to resist being ignored; it is almost impossible to tune the noise out, and for good reason. But to discover that built into the sound is also a trigger for us to become somehow better equipped to help them and react to their needs really is astonishing.[54]

But if you think that's clever, there's also evidence to suggest that babies also cry with a discernible accent from their very first week too. The cries of 60 babies born to French or German parents found that the children were crying with the same melody used in their native language. The French newborns ended their cries with a lilt at the end, as their Gallic mothers and fathers would, while the German tots started their cries intensely and dropped off at the end, which is akin to how their parents deliver sentences.[55]

What's more, the babies must have picked up their native melody while in the womb.

So to recap: when a baby cries it is impossible for you to ignore it. The sound itself produces a physical reaction in you that drives you to take action quickly and the melody is even delivered in a way you'll subconsciously find familiar.

You don't stand a chance.

So how in the world should we get this baby to sleep then?

The battle of bedtime

Before we get to the two main protagonists in these sleep wars, there are some global tricks and tips for getting your baby to snooze that don't generate quite so much controversy.

In Swiss maternity wards, for instance, newborns drift off in *Hängematten*, hammocks that bounce, rock and swing, and soothe the babies after their perilous journey into the world. Similarly, Filipina mothers use a *duyan* woven cradle to gently rock a tired babe until she drops off and her mother places her on the *banig*, or sleeping mat, for a nice long kip.

The Danes, Finns and Swedes have a long tradition of wrapping up their young and popping them outside for a fresh-air nap in their buggies. In fact, the Danish Health and Medicines Authority goes out of its way to recommend the practice, believing that babies sleep more soundly, eat with more gusto, and are more alert after a bracing outside sleep.

Then there's another Swedish tradition, known locally as 'buffing'. Parents lie their baby stomach down and then buff the baby's bottom, patting it firmly in a rhythmic motion until the child drifts off to sleep. The rhythmic bum patting is believed to bring back memories of the motion in the womb and provides a sense of security and safety, which brings with it some serious ZZZZZs.

Aside from these localised variations, though, it isn't an exaggeration to suggest that the world is split on how best to get our babies to sleep. You'd think that after the 6 or 7 million years we've been evolving as a species we'd have nailed something as fundamental and apparently simple as this, but not a bit of it.

The whole world of baby sleep has turned into an ideological battlefield in recent years, with the front line being largely in northern Europe, North America and Australia. On one side you have the co-sleepers and in the other the sleep trainers (including their paramilitary wing, the 'cry it out' brigade).

For the overwhelming majority of mothers and babies on the planet today, co-sleeping is an unquestioned fact of life. In much of southern Europe, Asia, Africa and Central and South America, mothers and babies sleep in the same bed, with many doing so until the babies are weaned and many more carrying on for long after that too.

There are differing styles and cultural quirks to be found, of course. Japanese parents often sleep in proximity with their children until they are three years old; in the Philippines and Vietnam some parents sleep with their baby in a hammock next to the bed. Others place their baby in a wicker basket in the bed between the two parents.

But whatever the circumstances, there are very few cultures in the world for which it would ever be thought acceptable or desirable to have babies sleeping alone.

There are plenty of co-sleeping advocates in northern Europe and North America too, of course, who point not only to its geographical dominance as a method, but also to claims that it leads to more independent, confident or outgoing children because of the bonds it builds and that the emotional security it fosters even results in children with higher self-esteem.

Why mess around with millennia of sleep technique? Well, there are a number of factors, it seems, that made certain parts of the Western world look elsewhere.

Firstly, co-sleeping and the often on-demand breastfeeding that can accompany it make huge demands on the mother. And while the baby may be in heaven, snoozing and dozing next to the person they love more than any other, for mothers, and indeed fathers, co-sleeping in the same bed or even room can often lead to very poor quality and fitful sleep. When one parent – or increasingly, in many industrialised economies, both – has to be up and out to work in the morning, this idyll starts to feel a lot less idyllic.

There's also a belief that independent sleeping makes for an independent child and adult, although there's very little evidence to back up that assertion. What does seem to have more veracity is the notion that babies who get themselves to sleep initially can do the same when and if they wake in the night.

Then there's the issue of sudden infant death syndrome (SIDS) or cot death. The link between co-sleeping and SIDS is a controversial and oft disputed one, but a recent *British Medical Journal* study stating that sharing a bed with a newborn increases the risk of SIDS fivefold – even if parents avoid other risk factors like tobacco, alcohol and drugs – put the practice into serious question for many. But it still has stanch support among its advocates, who essentially see it as the most natural thing in the world and point to places like Hong Kong, which has high rates of co-sleeping and a very low instance of cot death.

Thankfully, the advent of advice for parents not to put their children to sleep on their stomachs (despite this being exactly what was suggested in the preceding decades in many countries) has seen the SIDS rate fall across the globe.

Co-sleeping's potential link with SIDS, though, has parallels with the use of swaddling clothes to bind newborns. The New Testament has Jesus swaddled and various other sources mention it – baby wrapping has a 4,000 to 5,000-year-old history and was an almost ubiquitous part of helping your baby sleep up until the seventeenth century, when it began to fall out of favour. Despite its fall from grace, it still survives in many parts of the world, with countries such as Turkey still swaddling the vast majority of its newborns. There has also been something of a revival seen in the past decade in the UK and US too.

Like co-sleeping, swaddling has recently been linked with SIDS, and although subsequent studies have questioned that link, enough doubt has been placed in some parents' minds for them to give it a wide berth.

At the other end of the spectrum from the co-sleepers are parents who attempt to train their babies to sleep in a formalised way based around the establishment of routines.

Often a nightly, pre-sleep routine is part of the plan – a warm bath, a quiet cuddle and a final feed before bedtime, all of which ends up with baby falling asleep on their own with minimal distress and no nursing, rocking, bouncing, singing or face pulling.

Sounds great.

Except if it repeatedly doesn't work and your baby cries when put them down, you have a big choice to make – do you move on to the next level and let them 'cry it out'? In its harshest form, despite the bells and whistles that have been constructed around it in recent years, this essentially means your baby crying him- or herself to sleep enough times to realise that there's no point wailing any more, because, despite the occasional visit, no one is going to come and pick them up.

It's a tough business and not one that any parent enters into lightly, or if they do they certainly don't exit it unscathed.

As you can imagine, there couldn't be a starker difference between the co-sleepers and cry-it-outers, and online parenting forums in the UK and US especially are ablaze with often angry ideological debate around a subject that by its very nature attracts a lot of tired and cranky people to it!

Proponents believe that sleep training is the swiftest way to teach good sleep habits and have a calm, well-rested baby, as well as crucially providing an environment in which the whole family can sleep. The theory goes that in the modern world where everyone increasingly needs to work, a happy rested mum and dad will result in a happy baby, even if it was initially tough to make it happen. There's even early research to suggest that sleep training leads to less postnatal depression among mothers.

The theory goes that all babies cry, so if they need to shed a tear to develop such a worthwhile lifelong skill as sleeping well, then that's a price worth paying.

It's certainly proved to be an attractive alternative for many parents, although there's a concerning study that measured high levels of the stress hormone cortisol in distraught babies whose cries elicited no response from their parent or carer. Neurobiologists say that high cortisol levels are 'toxic' to the developing brain and that even when the baby appears to be settled much later, they still show the chemical signs of real stress.[56]

What's certain is that it's a very rare baby indeed who is born with the ability to self-soothe and fall into slumber without the touch or presence of their mother or father. In fact, the only time I've ever witnessed totally silent infants who had learned not to cry was in a neglected orphanage in Macedonia while the Kosovo war was being fought across the border – and that was because they knew no one would come, because no one ever had.

Driving the planet potty
Toilet training tips from the East

C ompared with the fractious debate around sleep, how the world toilet trains its young is a much softer world.

Kind of.

Beneath the 'baby need wee wee' cuteness of it all lies a reality that could have incredibly serious environmental implications for the lot of us.

A brief history of toilet training

In the beginning, every parent did the same thing, watching and waiting and training their young to learn to eliminate their waste when the time was right. This was exclusively driven by a health imperative – toilet waste spreads diseases and eventually kills, so teaching children at as young an age as possible to go when and where was most hygienic didn't just make sense, it was a key part of our continued survival as a species.

It wasn't until around 1600 in England that the first traces of what we now know as a nappy or diaper came into being, and even then it was far from an overnight sensation as it was riotously expensive. And for those who had trained their children up until that point, without the use of anything other than repeated encouragement and practice, the nappy was an unnecessary inconvenience rather than the exact opposite as it is seen in many parts of the world today.

As we will see, the expense of nappies (and then the social status that comes with being able to afford the disposability of them) together with the time and attention needed to toilet train children at a very early age have been the big drivers in creating the situation we find ourselves in today, when an estimated 50% of the world's children are toilet trained by the time they turn one, with the majority of those being trained without the use of a nappy – and the other half wearing disposable diapers for an increasingly longer time.[57]

Before we look into how different cultures approach this issue, we need to see how the interventions of two men also had a bearing on how the industrialised West especially left early toilet training behind and began to put nappies on their children until they were old enough to consciously participate in their own mastery of toilet skills.

In the early part of the twentieth century, the father of psychoanalysis, Sigmund Freud, postulated that negative reactions from parents when toilet training can lead to an anally retentive personality. If parents forced children to learn to control their bowel movements before they were good and ready, they could unwittingly foster a deliberate holding back as a form of rebellion, and the child would develop into an adult who hated mess, adored order and tidiness, never questioned authority, was tight with money and dreadfully stubborn.

Go too far the other way, though, said Freud, and your liberal 'go where you want' toilet training will bring about a messy, rebellious adult who doesn't give two hoots about other people's feelings.

It's enough to make you not want to go at all. Ever.

Chicago psychoanalyst Robert Galatzer-Levy has since suggested that toilet training was high on Freud's agenda because he lived at a time before indoor plumbing when large households battled for a go on the chamber pot or waited for the freezing-cold outhouse to become free – but the die had been cast.[58]

This view was reinforced in Dr Benjamin Spock's *Baby and Child Care* published in 1946 – a book so successful and influential on generations of parents that it is reputed to have been outsold only by the Bible in its first 50 years in print. Spock was the first paediatrician to study the psychoanalysis of Freud to try to understand children's needs. As part of his incredibly well-received guidance, he recommended against any form of toilet training in the first year, believing, as Freud had suggested, that it could lead to rebellion later through bedwetting.

So, as prosperity in the industrialised West saw more nappies appear and psychoanalysis seeded a sense that later was better where potty training was concerned, so the divide opened up in how we as a planet trained our young to do what needs to be done and we arrive at the almost fifty–fifty split we have today – although that parity is about to change in a big way.

Planet Potty today

In the shanty towns of East Africa, the favelas of Latin America and the crowded slums of India's cities you see some sights – but washing lines full of towelling nappies or mounds of disposable diapers aren't one of them.

In these and other societies, including much of rural South East Asia and parts of Central Europe, parents, and especially mothers, learn to recognise their babies' body signals in the first weeks of life and use them to anticipate when their babies need to expel waste.

When they judge the infant is ready to go, they hold the baby over a sink, bowl, toilet, open ground or wherever and whatever is available and safe. They then use a sound or gesture to encourage and gently condition the baby to go when in this situation and only this situation.

It's simple but it works.

The baby learns to associate this sign or noise with going to the toilet and soon the signal becomes an invitation or request to go. Babies in the first year of their lives obviously can't wipe themselves, so these first forays are more about staying dry and clean with parental help than they are about going to the toilet independently.

This early infant toilet training is necessarily a more modest affair, with nappies not a financial option, but hygiene is often of the utmost importance in environments where disease can spread like wildfire. It is a method that's tried, tested and still practised across great swathes of the planet.

The relatively speedy move from toilet training children within the first few months of their lives to using nappies and waiting until they are two, three or four, as is the case now, has also led to a clash of intergenerational cultures in places such as the UK. Grandparents who did things very differently in their day often raise an eyebrow at what they see as an expensive example of progress doing us a major disservice.

It's a similar story across much of Western Europe and in the United States too. In the US, past generations would have seen most children out of diapers by 18 months,[59] whereas a recent study showed that more than half the children over 32 months failed to stay dry during the day. Put simply, post-war prosperity has resulted in children in the West taking longer and longer to learn how to go to the toilet – and as relatively uncomfortable towelling nappies have been superseded by super-comfortable and dry disposables, the imperative to go to the toilet has slipped later and later. For many a parent, the onset of nursery and school at four or five years old is now seen as the hard stop in terms of when youngsters need to be fully toilet trained.[60]

Does it really matter, though? So what if many of today's kids wear nappies for a year or two or three?

According to studies it does matter. Later toilet training is associated with an increased risk of urinary and bowel problems, like urinary tract infections and lack of bladder control.[61]

And then, of course, there's the environmental factor. With the average baby going through up to 8,000 disposable nappies and each one taking up to 200 years to biodegrade, you can see why the landfill implications are enormous – and the situation could be about to get an awful lot worse.

Since time immemorial the Chinese have employed an early toilet training technique that uses no nappies, just hard (usually maternal) work, instinct and perseverance. Special split crotch pants called *kaidangku* are utilised along with an anytime, anywhere approach, with little ones held over where they need to go. The parental trigger noise is made, and before you know it Chinese babies, in their cute little trousers, are toilet trained.

But this is changing and it has huge implications.

As urban Chinese parents become more cash rich and time poor, they are increasingly swapping the split pants for disposable diapers. As well as the convenience factor, being able to use and discard an item is also an outward sign of wealth. It's already estimated that China accounts for 14% of all nappy use globally, and even at this early stage it represents Pampers' second largest market after the USA.[62]

The only place on earth with more babies' bottoms to consider than China is India, another country with a long tradition of early, pretty much nappy-less, toilet training. But, as economic progress is being made, there too the disposable diaper is creeping in.

Time will tell if China and India get the disposable nappy bug quite as badly as the West. The irony is that the early toilet training method – rebranded and jargonised as 'elimination communication'– is beginning to take off in the US and UK. Washable cloth nappies have been making a comeback too.

Planet Potty, like Planet Parent, just keeps on turning!

A parent's perspective

Oak – China

Our daughter is two months old and my wife and I believe she should enjoy her nappies like many other infants her age in China nowadays.

However, my mother-in-law strongly suggested that we try the baby potty. She believes, as do many of her generation, that the earlier we train our daughter to use it, the better and easier it will be for everyone.

So basically, after her one-month celebration, her grandmother put her on the potty and whistled! This is a technique that is very common in China, especially among the older generation. When you feel that the baby is already in the right position and ready to pee, he or she will start to whistle – a gentle, soft whistle, which is like the sound of peeing.

In time this noise makes the baby excited and ready to pee, and eventually they are able to control when they need to go before they are even one year old.

Despite being a bit suspicious of the whistling way, I can see already that it really does work!

WORLDLY WISDOM - LOOKING AFTER BABY

Snobbery or social science? Whatever's behind it, there's enough evidence across the planet to suggest that the name you are given really can have an impact on your life.

As parental decisions go, it's a biggy.

Research in the US shows that even by the age of seven, children with the worst sleep patterns exhibit the highest rates of obesity and body fat, including abdominal fat, which is believed to be associated with heart disease and diabetes.

Sleep training, or letting your baby cry itself to sleep, is one of the most fiercely debated issues in early parenthood. For much of the planet, demand feeding and often co-sleeping still rule the roost. But in the industrialised West, the 'crying it out' method has gained real ground.

Studies showing high levels of the stress hormone cortisol in distraught babies whose cries elicited no response from a parent or carer sit next to others that say that, in the long run, no harm is done.

An estimated 50% of the world's children are toilet trained by the time they turn one, with the majority of those being trained without the use of a single nappy.

The other half of the planet is increasingly using disposable nappies and seeing its children wearing them for a longer and longer time.

4
Food

There's perhaps nothing that gives me a more immediate, pure, yet deep-rooted sense of primeval pleasure than watching my children eat.

As a parent it feels like one of your primary functions is to ensure that your offspring take on board what they need to survive.

Initially, of course, this is all down to you as guardians to provide, judge and monitor the nutritional intake of your helpless baby, but as they grow this task becomes about instilling habits that will provide a blueprint for a long and healthy life.

Or at least that's the theory.

Eating may be as fundamental a function as it's possible to imagine, but with the importance it wields comes a responsibility that can often begin to weigh incredibly heavily when things don't go to plan.

From breastfeeding and school meals to the scourge of childhood obesity sitting side by side with infant malnutrition, the world and its children are fighting a battle on a number of food-related fronts.

Of bottles and breastfeeds

Who does what on the great milk merry-go-round?

I n certain parts of Planet Parent there's one issue that is the cause of more debate, more anxiety and often more anger than almost any other – breastfeeding.

For an action as old as we are as a species, you might be forgiven for thinking that a coalescing of opinions around it may have taken place these past 10,000 years or so, that we would have sorted out our differences either way and now just kind of – well, you know – get on with it.

Not a bit of it.

From the breast versus bottle debate, to those who have chosen the former but then have to negotiate the minefield of when and where it's permissible to actually do it, giving our very young the nourishment they need has become a battlefield.

It's a mistake to think it's only in the modern world that breastfeeding has become a complicated issue; the history of how we feed our young tells us an awful lot about how we've ended up where we are today.

The milky way

The engagement of a wet nurse – the definition of which is a woman who breastfeeds another's child – seems perverse to most people now, a historical quirk from a dim and distant past. It was far from a flash in the pan, though, having begun as early as 2000 BC and lasting well into the last century.

Throughout this huge timespan, wet nursing evolved from being something turned to in times of need into essentially a lifestyle choice. For hundreds of years it represented a bona fide profession with contracts and laws to regulate its practice.

It wasn't until the introduction of the feeding bottle in the nineteenth century and the birth of the formula arms race that the practice began to fade away, as we will see.

What had driven the creation of the wet nurse industry was that then, as now, women didn't always find it easy or possible to lactate and feed. In fact, lactation failure is mentioned in the very earliest medical encyclopaedia, the Egyptian Ebers Papyrus, in 1550 BC, which even gave this treatment as a potential cure:

> 'To get a supply of milk in a woman's breast for suckling a child: Warm the bones of a swordfish in oil and rub her back with it. Or: Let the woman sit cross-legged and eat fragrant bread of soused durra, while rubbing the parts with the poppy plant.'[63]

Obvious really.

By the time we reach Greece in around 950 BC, women of high social status were frequently demanding wet nurses in a 'too fancy to feed' kind of way.

Our old 'no pun intended' friend Soranus of Ephesus, the father of obstetrics and gynaecology, wrote an ancient guide to all things wet nursing including a fingernail test for assessing the quality and consistency of breast milk. A drop of breast milk placed on the fingernail should not be watery enough to run off or thick enough to stick when the hand is turned upside down – a method that remained in common use for 1,500 years.

A wet nurse wasn't just about feeding, though. Jumping forward a millennium or so, Bartholomeus Anglicus, a Franciscan friar, listed in the 1240s some of these qualities and duties of the wet nurse:

> '*A nurse rejoices with a boy when it rejoices and weeps with him when he weeps, just like a mother. She picks him up when he falls, gives the little one milk when he cries, kisses him as he lies, holds him tight and gathers him up when he sprawls, washes and cleans the little one when he makes a mess of himself.*'[64]

Supernanny, if ever there was one.

During the Middle Ages, the belief began to take hold that breast milk could somehow pass on both the physical and mental traits of the wet nurse herself and eventually a return was seen to mothers feeding their own young.

In the early seventeenth century, the French obstetrician Jacques Guillemeau proposed four main objections to a wet nurse: 1) the child may be switched with another put in its place; 2) the affection felt between the child and the mother will diminish; 3) a bad condition may be inherited by the child; and 4) the nurse may transmit an imperfection of her own body to the child that could then be transmitted to the parents.

If, added Guillemeau, a wet nurse was needed on medical grounds, redheads were to be avoided because they were known to have a hot temperament that was harmful to their breast milk.[65]

Despite this growing groundswell of negativity, it took a while for the practice to fully die out, with aristocratic women still keen to avoid doing the feeding themselves because it was considered unfashionable, bad for the figure and a pain when it came to social activities. Then, at the other end of the social spectrum, the Industrial Revolution saw many working-class women needing to work to meet the rising cost of living (yes even then), meaning they were forced to give their children to local peasant women to be fed.

By 1900, the wet-nursing profession was all but dead. But is it on the way back?

In the last few years, wet nursing has had something of a resurgence. Of course, it will have been occurring informally where needed, especially in developing countries, but in the US in particular wet nursing as a paid-for service is back.[66]

Generating headlines about how the 'too posh to push' brigade are now too busy to breastfeed, its comeback seems to be driven primarily by those with money but not the time or inclination to breastfeed for themselves.

For the overwhelmingly vast majority of mothers on Planet Parent, though, if for whatever reason breastfeeding isn't an option, the alternative is bottle-shaped.

Hitting the bottle

Bottle-feeding is older than you think.

Clay feeding vessels dating from 2000 BC onwards have been found that chemical tests show to have contained animal milk, but it wasn't until the Industrial Revolution that things really kicked off with the pewter bubby pot invented in 1770 by Hugh Smith, a canny doctor at Middlesex Hospital in London.

Looking very much like a coffee pot and with a small rag tied over the spout holes to act as the business end of things, this little rudimentary device started the product development chain that led to the array of weird and wonderful bottles you see before you in baby stores today.

Although I doubt any beat 'bubby pot' as a brand name.

Tragically, though, just as we've seen with childbirth at that time, the lack of understanding about bacteria and infection meant that because these early devices were hard to clean properly, it's estimated that one-third of all artificially fed infants during that period died within their first year of life.

But as the modern feeding bottle and artificial teat were refined and remodelled, first using glass and rubber and then plastic, artificial feeding began to really gain traction in the industrialised West and soon medicine started to look beyond animal milk towards an alternative source of liquid nutrition for babies.

Using animal milk to feed babies had been recorded as far back as 2000 BC. The type of milk used depended, of course, on the kind of animal around at the time, with goats, sheep, donkeys, camels, pigs and horses all having been called upon, but with cows becoming the predominant choice.

In the eighteenth century things changed. French doctor Jean Charles Des-Essartz published his *Treatise of Physical Upbringing of Children* in 1760 and for the first time looked at the composition of human milk compared with that of animals. Based on chemical characteristics, Des-Essartz justified human milk as the best source, setting off a train of scientific endeavour to attempt to create a substitute that resembled the milk produced by human mothers as closely as possible.

The race for the formula was on.

In 1865, chemist Justus von Liebig marketed an infant food of cows' milk, wheat, malt flour and potassium bicarbonate and held it up as the perfect infant food.

It wasn't.

As with many of its immediate successors, it was fattening all right, but it was bereft of essential nutrients like protein, vitamins and minerals – a shortfall that was eventually overcome via fortification.

By the late 1800s, brands such as Nestlé's Food, Horlick's Malted Milk and Robinson's Patent Barley were all vying for their share of this new, lucrative market, and as the appetite grew so did the endorsements. In the US, 1929 saw the American Medical Association (AMA) form the Committee on Foods to approve the safety and quality of formula, and by the 1940s and 1950s powdered baby milk had entered the mainstream in the States and a corporate machine was well and truly in motion.

The marketing of formulas became more sophisticated and aggressive, not just in the US and other industrialised nations, but also in developing countries by the likes of Nestlé, which has attracted much criticism for the practice. A global decline in breastfeeding has now occurred, with the global breastfeeding rate of 90% in the twentieth century estimated to be just 42% in the twenty-first.[67]

But does it really matter?

Breastfeeding versus formula-feeding

Let's cut to the chase: nutritionally, breast is best.

The notion that in a couple of hundred years or so we could synthetically manufacture what evolution has taken millennia to perfect was always going to be hard to swallow in more ways than one.

But that's not the only evidence on offer. In fact, the list is almost endless.

It is estimated that non-exclusive breastfeeding in the first six months of life results in 1.4 million deaths and 10% of the disease burden is in children younger than five years. Research also shows increasing trends of formula-fed children developing diabetes and childhood obesity.[68]

Save the Children recommends that formula milk packaging should carry huge, cigarette-style health warnings stating that 95 babies could be saved every hour worldwide if new mothers breastfed immediately after birth.

The breastfeeding of infants under two years of age also has the greatest potential impact on child survival of all preventive interventions. Breastfeeding has the potential to prevent over 800,000 deaths in children under five in the developing world and a breastfed child in a developing nation has at least six times more chance of survival in the early months than a non-breastfed one. Plus, an exclusively breastfed child is 14 times less likely to die in their first six months.

Without doubt, a huge contributing factor in those shocking statistics revolves around the practical nightmare bottle-feeding often constitutes for mothers in developing countries. Ensuring that the formula is mixed with safe water, that the mixture proportion is correct and that feeding utensils are sufficiently clean is next to impossible in many of the world's poorest countries.

Don't imagine this is an issue that excludes the West, though.

In the United States, a survey found a 25% increase in mortality among non-breastfed infants; in the UK's Millennium Cohort Survey, six months of exclusive breastfeeding was associated with a 53% decrease in hospital admissions for diarrhoea and a 27% decrease in respiratory tract infections.

The benefits aren't only confined to the child, either; breastfeeding has also been found to contribute to maternal health immediately after the delivery by reducing the risk of postpartum haemorrhage and to reducing type 2 diabetes as well as breast, uterine and ovarian cancer.

Studies have even found an association between stopping feeding too early and postnatal depression in mothers.

OK, OK, OK, enough already. Point taken.

So why does France have the lowest breastfeeding rate in the Western world then?

The fact that the book *The Conflict: Woman and Mother*, which warns that breastfeeding is a Trojan horse rolling back the gains of the women's movement and shackling women to 'despotic, gluttonous babies who devour their mothers', was a French parenting bestseller a year or two ago is a pointer.

The French author and philosopher Elisabeth Badinter also advises that women beat back their babies with bottles of formula milk and install rigid feeding regimes if they are to retain their independence and that French women are being bombarded by the 'breast is best' propaganda, which is designed to make them feel guilty for not overcoming their 'disgust' at the notion of putting baby to breast.

That kind of diatribe is fairly typical of a debate that has become increasingly fractious on both sides, particularly in France but way beyond there too.

The extreme 'breast is best' brigade denounce the bottle, while the formula gang hurl back earth mother insults.

In the middle, somewhere, cowers the fact that breast may well be best, but not every mother produces enough milk to sate her baby. My own mother, after six preceding children before all 9lbs 2 of me arrived, was one who just ran out of milk and turned to the bottle, as it were.

When it comes to the art of latching and breastfeeding technique, many, many mothers have a torrid time too and have the first days and weeks of motherhood reduced to a painful nightmare as they struggle on.

Breastfeeding might well be natural, but it's far from easy, and if a mother who can't breastfeed for whatever reason has ready access to formula milk and needs to use it, surely that is a reason to thank our lucky stars?

The most sensible voice on the entire debate I know is that of Clare Byam-Cook, a former nurse, midwife and breastfeeding counsellor:

> *'Lots of mothers don't produce enough milk. Not just a significant minority – loads. In the old days, mothers who didn't produce enough milk either went to the village wet nurse and begged for milk, or they had malnourished babies. It's not a modern problem.'*

So we're all agreed. If formula is for you, that's great. If breast feels best, then wherever you are on Planet Parent, go for it.

Oh. Hold on a second . . .

Breastfeeding in public

To say there's global variation in the attitudes towards breastfeeding in public would be an enormous understatement.

What's more, there's a cultural anomaly running right through the complex patchwork of rules and taboos around where and when women can breastfeed with impunity (if they so desire).

In Africa, for example, the situation changes from country to country, region to region. Egyptian women by and large cannot breastfeed in public, but in Ghana, Kenya, Uganda and Zambia for the most part they most certainly can. Even though the culture in many of these countries frowns upon exposing the body in public, breastfeeding is seen as a natural and acceptable exception.

Likewise in Bangladesh, Sri Lanka, Nepal and India – all societies where public nudity is socially unacceptable by and large, but public feeding, carried out with relative modesty, generally isn't a problem.

Even in Pakistan, Iran and parts of Afghanistan, where most women cover up, publicly nursing your infant is generally accepted – albeit with many mothers choosing to partially cover themselves with a scarf.

The irony is, though, that when we begin to look at much of Europe, North America and Australia, territories with a much more laissez-faire attitude towards flesh being on show in general, opinions on public breastfeeding begin to harden and even turn rather nasty.

It's not that women are outlawed from feeding in front of others – in fact, many countries enshrine the right in law – it's that they can come under verbal and now virtual attack for doing so.

In the UK, for instance, in recent years breastfeeding in public has become a far more contentious issue than it was even a decade ago. So much so that the head of the Royal College of Midwives recently declared that the level of abuse given out to women for daring to breastfeed in public is causing many to give up altogether.

And there have been some pretty unsavoury recent examples too.

A woman in the UK was photographed feeding her eight-month-old daughter while sitting outside and found the image posted on Facebook with a caption declaring her a 'tramp', and another mother found herself shunted out of a hospital waiting room and into a private office for daring to do the same.

The deputy editor of the leading UK parenting magazine even went as far as to describe breastfeeding as 'creepy', adding that seeing her baby where only a lover had been before made her opt for the bottle option.

Nursing mothers are fighting back, though, and a new poster campaign from students at the University of North Texas has gained worldwide viral momentum thanks to its impactful images of breastfeeding mothers being forced to use toilet cubicles rather than sit in the open.

The 'When Nurture Calls' campaign, which was designed by art students at the university, seems to have really hit a nerve, as has a spoof song from Down Under, 'Ruin Your Day'. The catchy number was inspired when a mother of four from Canberra was breastfeeding her youngest child in a café and another customer felt it well within their rights to utter a disparaging comment under their breath.

The video, which pokes fun at people who get offended by new mothers doing what many new mothers need to do, has proved that the time may be right to turn the tide. It racked up more than 800,000 online views and was translated into 10 different languages within a month of being published.

The final word should perhaps go to a somewhat unlikely source, Pope Francis, a pontiff who is turning out to be unafraid of confronting an issue or two. During a special papal baptism, the Argentinian said that mothers 'should not stand on ceremony' if their children were hungry. 'If they are hungry, mothers, feed them, without thinking twice, because they are the most important people here.'

One more mouthful
What do the world's children eat?

S o, then, what do the planet's children eat? The answer seems to be anything and everything if left to their own devices.

OK, they might not all eat everything, but collectively the planet's children have a pretty good go at almost every type of food you can imagine.

In the Arctic, for instance, a traditional Inuit diet during spells when food is scarce and the bitter cold makes preparation impossible can consist of *maktak* – whale skin and blubber – and *qisaruaq* – chewed cud retrieved from a slaughtered caribou's stomach.

Tuck in kids.

Which, of course, they do. Although interestingly the Inuit uniformly report that if they don't get the youngsters chewing on the old whale blubber and regurgitated pap before they are two or three years old, you've lost them forever – a theory that chimes somewhat with the much heralded French way of feeding children, as we are about to see.

Traditional Taiwanese kids' favourites include fish eyes, dried cuttlefish, fried anchovies, jellyfish, sea cucumber and eel, and I've seen children in East Africa happily chewing on toasted crickets (bug eating has been tipped to be the answer to global food crises, given that they are rich in protein and about as abundant as it gets). Japanese youngsters demolish every type of sushi and I once had a conversation with a boy from Chennai about black pudding during which he not unreasonably asked me in all seriousness if Britain was a nation of vampires given our obvious taste for blood-based cuisine.

While children do develop their palates along with everything else they've got going on, the notion that they will only stomach food without notable taste or texture doesn't stand up to global scrutiny.

So why are great swathes of Europe feeding their children nut-based chocolate spread for breakfast? And how come British and American youngsters would choose coco pops and pop tarts of a morning over almost any savoury option?

Where has this seemingly all-conquering sweet tooth come from all of a sudden?

Actually, it's been quite a long time in the making.

Fruits of the forest

While our tongues can detect basic flavours – salt, sour, bitter and sweet – it's the latter that has always rocked our boats the most.

Our primate ancestors spent their days in the forest searching for ripe, sweet fruit. When they were lucky enough to find a bush laden with the stuff, they stripped it clean.

After all, who knew when they'd come across another mother lode?

Sweet, ripe fruit meant more energy, and natural selection rewarded whoever recognised that fact. Which means that you and me and every other human on the planet are all programmed to be really good at finding and eating sweet stuff.

Really, really good.

It doesn't just stop at fruit, of course. Our close cousins the chimps have been observed not only using sticks to delve into beehives to get at honey, but also viewing painful stings as a price well worth paying for a drop of the sweet stuff.

Once Homo sapiens had wandered out of the forest, we didn't waste much time domesticating sugar cane and later learning how to extract the sugar from beets and corn so we could grow it in almost whatever climate zone we found ourselves in.

There was no turning back. Gone were the days when we happened across an occasional stash of berries; we could have sugar with everything and, much like the chimps who take on stings at the bees' nest, the consequences could go hang.

Who needed teeth anyway?

As the food industry was quick to discover, if you put a little – or substantially more than a little – sweetness in almost any product, people like it more. A lot more.

So they did and still do, with glucose-fructose syrup, also known as high fructose corn syrup, one of the key ingredients in today's high-tech food production sector.

This corn derivative, which is processed using enzymes to convert its glucose into fruit sugar, was developed in the 1950s but became popular after quotas and tariffs imposed on imported sugar in the late 1970s drove food manufacturers to seek an alternative. The synthetic corn sweetener was that alternative, and both Coca-Cola and Pepsi, among others, switched from sugar to high fructose corn syrup in their US production processes in the 1980s.

It's cheaper than regular cane sugar, sweet as sweet can be, and because corn is grown everywhere, it's everywhere too. Not only is it cheap and plentiful, it also helps keep foods moist, boosting shelf life as well as providing texture and crunch to biscuits and thickening up ice cream and yoghurt.

In short, it's a manufacturer's dream.

Listed as 'glucose-fructose syrup', 'high fructose corn syrup', 'HFCS' or under other increasingly oblique names, it's becoming harder and harder to avoid loading your shopping trolley up with products containing it. As a consequence, our children are becoming more and more exposed to it and it's suspected of playing a part in creating the full-scale global weight epidemic that we will look at later.

But all is not lost – the world's parents haven't thrown in the towel yet and there are some fantastic dishes, approaches and techniques out there that can help us all to encourage our children not only to enjoy food but to enjoy food that helps them thrive.

Thought for food

The Japanese enjoy the world's longest average lifespans and there's a big argument to say that part of the reason is the fact that they get their children eating good food from a very young age.

Rice or noodles form the staple of most toddler meals, with fish, meat and vegetables all offered up to enhance the flavour. Egg rice with grilled fish is probably the most regularly made youngsters' meal in the country and nutritionally it ticks many a box and avoids the processed food jungle that can lead to so many problems and can establish lifelong and eventually life-threatening bad habits.

In fact, fish is more popular than meat in Japan and South Korea because it's said there's so much nearby sea to plunder. It's a rational argument, but Britain is surrounded by some of the most fertile waters on the planet and our consumption rate of fresh fish – battered cod aside – is woeful, especially where children are concerned.

Even when it comes to a sweet treat, traditional Japanese cooking puts the *kimi* ball up for grabs, an egg-flavoured, rice flour-based sugary treat that might sound a little odd to the uninitiated but apparently melts in the mouth and is a big hit with Japan's discerning young eaters.

Danish children, just like many of their Scandinavian counterparts, love a meatball, but it's the *smørrebrød*, an open-faced sandwich made with rye or pumpernickel bread, that they really go wild for. Fillings include, among other things, liverwurst, cod roe and mackerel (fish heavy again).

As we're becoming accustomed to seeing on our journey around Planet Parent so far, the Swedes top a disproportionately large number of international league tables and here's perhaps the most surprising one. When it comes to ketchup consumption, Sweden is number one – and children play a big part in that stellar success by putting red sauce on almost everything.

In India, Bangladesh and parts of Pakistan, *khichdi* (which is the inspiration for kedgeree) is king of the kids' menu. A mushy rice and lentil-based dish, it has the look of a porridge that has been transformed by turmeric. Add in vegetables as well as goat, lamb or chicken plus a twist of lime or a dab of pickled mango and you're done.

I'm imagining you're quite hungry now.

What if I told you that other childhood favourites in that region include *aloo gobi*, a mild potato and cauliflower curry, *pakora*, lightly fried veg parcels and *naan* bread or *chapatti*?

Starving?

In Israel, toddlers are soon full card-carrying members of the olive appreciation society, with an olive and butter sandwich being a particular favourite. Turkish parents make a popular children's lunchtime dish called *sebze yemegi*, a simple but effective way of getting good food packed with nutrients into a young diner. Take whatever vegetables are in season – celery, peas, green beans, spinach, artichokes, courgettes, whatever you can find at the market – add white or brown rice, bulgur wheat, red lentils, minced chicken, lamb or beef, and serve with a side salad and natural yoghurt.

Delicious, filling and fresh, and can be made in bulk and frozen for parents who just haven't got the time to cook from scratch each day – a problem that is routinely cited as a barrier to getting busy in the kitchen.

The proliferation of fast food has gone hand in hand with increasing levels of time poverty among parents, something that's particularly true in South Korea. The wonderful traditional Korean cuisine still remains, of course, with children developing an early taste for the spicy, vibrant flavours that dominate it. *Kimchi*, a pickled vegetable dish containing cabbage, radish, garlic, onions and sometimes seafood, is a very popular child pleaser, as is *kimbap*, rice and small portions of vegetables wrapped in seaweed sheets.

So, despite the fast food and even faster lifestyles, the world does feed its children a huge range of dishes that have a myriad of flavours and textures – and they get eaten.

As well as the food itself, of course, there's the approach to serving it up too. Should I really be calling calamari 'octopus chips' as a sneaky ploy (successful, as it happens) to get my children to first try them and then love them?

Is the 'no pudding until you've cleared your plate' approach of old a wise one?

There's one country on Planet Parent that seems to have really cracked it when it comes to how their children eat, and in recent years the techniques themselves have become something of a cultural export.

Vive la différence

The French have always prided themselves on being, well, French. Their sense of other, of difference, has on occasion been interpreted as arrogance by others or even as a *c'est la vie* sense of isolationism that says 'we are happy being us and doing what we do'. Only in French.

In the last few years, especially in the area of food, the French way has been dissected and disseminated, with other nations desperate to know how the French seem to eat so well and stay relatively slim.

A large part of this cultural cuisine curtain twitching has revolved around the process of ensuring that French children don't just eat well, but also develop a positive, adventurous and healthy overall attitude to food at a very early age.

We've already seen that France has one of the lowest breastfeeding rates in the world, so once they've had their fill of formula at six months or so, what are they weaned on? Do they go straight to onion soup and soufflé?

Not quite, no. But they do have a different approach to almost anywhere else. The French Society of Paediatrics recommends what it calls 'food diversification', which essentially means parents introducing a different vegetable to their child every four days or so once solids come into play. By and large they do just that, with a study showing that on average 40% of babies are introduced to between seven and 12 vegetables by the time they are one.[69]

The rationale revolves around the notion of developing the child's taste by exposure to as many flavours as possible before they reach the age of two, when, according to the French authorities, the level of appetite falls and a reticence about trying new foods begins to rear its head.

This essentially creates a race to accustom French children to as many veggie flavours as possible before the drawbridge drops and little ones begin to say '*Non!*'

So then, what's cooking?

First there are potatoes, which often form a base to be mixed with carrots, pumpkin, green beans, leeks, spinach and courgettes as well as baby endive and chard.

And that's just for starters. Taking in the complex flavours on offer in the pureed baby food aisle in a French hypermarket is a thing of wonder indeed.

While many Western countries have seen a move to baby-led weaning based on the child picking up finger foods and encountering taste and texture at the same time, the French, it may not surprise you to hear, fundamentally disagree.

Eating chunky foods is seen by most French parents as an almost guaranteed way to make very young children steer clear of more adventurous foods for life. Much better, they say, to get them into all sorts of tastes and the texture will take care of itself later.

As children reach school age, this method of normalising all sorts of tastes and flavours continues with a school meal system that puts most others around the developed world to shame. Food education is seen as a priority, not a refuelling session between proper lessons, and in both the classroom and the dining hall delicious food is discussed and celebrated.

From the age of three, school lunch is an event – much as any and every mealtime is treated by the French, in fact. It's common to find three or even four courses on offer: a vegetable starter, a hot main course served with vegetables, a cheese course and dessert, which more often than not is fruit, with a sweet treat being on the menu just once a week or so. The main meals can range from veal, ratatouille or grilled fish to sautéed chicken, chèvre salad or even (that's an Anglo-Saxon-inspired 'even' rather than a Gallic one, of course) escargot.

Why not? It's food, it's delicious and, in terms of life skills, learning to love intrinsically fresh and healthy food must be up there with the most important of all.

Water is the only drink available (all vending machines were banned in French schools in 2005) and for the main course there is only one choice on the menu until children turn 12. Like it or lump it. Also until they are 12, food is served to the children at the table and they are required to sit and eat for at least 30 minutes.

Compared with France, many other developed nations' school meal offerings read poorly, with most in the USA, for example, feeling much more like a fast-food menu than a brasserie. Nearby Britain has begun the process of following suit; in 2014, regulations were introduced that meant all schools are required by law to serve one or more portions of vegetables or salad a day, wholegrain carbohydrates, water as the main drink, and no more than two portions a week of food that has been deep-fried or battered – and that includes pastry.

Perhaps the most fundamental rule and important lesson that runs through the entire Gallic method when it comes to children and food is about tasting. No French child is expected to eat all of the artichoke hearts on their plate, but they are expected to at least try them, to take just a bite.

Getting over that fear of the unfamiliar is key. Once it has been beaten, kids may not like everything straight away, but they will come round to liking most things in time because they will be happy to keep trying them.

As if to back up this approach further, research has recently found that encouraging children to eat everything on their plate could actually lead to the type of unhealthy relationship with food that can result in overeating later in life![70]

Can everyone go French, though? Well, the global paradox is that many poorer nations feed their children better than the world's richest. On a visit to an HIV/Aids project on the outskirts of Johannesburg a decade ago, I witnessed a delicious stew being made for the children, many of whom would get only one meal that day, using fresh seasonal root vegetables, stock and seasoning. It was tasty, simple and utterly nutritious. Also there that day, as something so healthy was created by those with so little, was chef Jamie Oliver. The experience spurred him on to create his School Dinners campaign, which not only highlighted the issue of what the world's schools were feeding its pupils, but also, in time, led to legislation change in the UK. Oliver's initial campaign was shown to have improved not only school meal menus but also grades and attendance levels too.[71]

Imagine what the fantastic food on offer in French schools does for their kids.

As we will see, though, it's often when prosperity and development really take hold that the door is opened wide to obesity. So this isn't really about resources, it's about attitude, culture, habit and will.

While the French model might not be workable everywhere, the sentiment behind it – introducing young children to different tastes and taking the time and effort to establish in them the importance of good food – is far from being an idiosyncratic quirk that the rest of the world sees as being typically French. We need to change the way we all teach our children to eat – because something very grave is happening right in front of our eyes.

Obesity
Everyone's problem

The growth of growth

When finding myself talking to a group of Brazilians living in a favela in Rio de Janeiro, exactly a week before the 2014 World Cup began, I imagined the moment they clocked I was from England there would be only one topic of conversation.

Wayne Rooney's preferable starting position maybe? Perennial penalty taking problems? Or perhaps the fact that the nation that invented the planet's favourite game had been crowned world champions of it only once?

Whatever the finer details, it felt an odds-on certainty that football would be the topic to bridge any cultural divides that existed between us.

But no. What we found ourselves talking about was obesity, and specifically a story that had broken in the UK days earlier and had seemingly struck a chord on the back streets of Brazil too.

It had been reported that an 11-year-old boy from Norfolk was 5ft 1in tall and 15 stone, with a body mass index (BMI) of 41.8. Obesity is measured at 30 or greater, with a normal BMI lower than 25.

It's a sad tale for sure, but certainly not an unusual one, not even in Rio, where a street away from the bronzed bodies of Ipanema and the city's other famous beaches, people, especially the city's poorest people, are as much in the grip of the obesity epidemic as anywhere else on the planet.

What made this story really stand out, though, was the fact that the parents of the child were arrested by the police on suspicion of cruelty and neglect, solely because their child was so overweight.

Obesity puts children at increased risk of high cholesterol, cardiovascular disease, high blood pressure, diabetes, certain cancers, and mental and emotional issues. This is serous stuff, and the fact that this couple were being held legally responsible for bringing all that upon their son gained an awful lot of global attention because this really is a truly global issue.

Because the phrase 'obesity epidemic' has been bandied about for years now, it somehow feels like it has lost some of its meaning and impact. But a glance at the table below showing the percentage of adults considered obese in the world's developed countries makes it very clear that this modern curse cuts across all boundaries.

The numbers make for very grim reading all round, and no country has succeeded in reducing obesity rates, resulting in a world where the number of overweight and obese adults has almost quadrupled to around 1 billion since 1980. That represents a global growth in the overweight and obese from 23% of the world's population in 1980 to 34% in 2008.[72]

That truly is an epidemic.

What's more, the bulk of this increase was seen in the developing world, particularly in countries where incomes were rising like Egypt and Mexico, a state of affairs that signals catastrophic trouble ahead if

The prevalence of obesity among adults in developed countries[73]

Rank	Country	% obese
1	Mexico	32.8
2	United States	31.8
3	Syria	31.6
4	Venezuela	30.8
4	Libya	30.8
6	Trinidad and Tobago	30.0
7	Vanuatu	29.8
8	Iraq	29.4
8	Argentina	29.4
10	Turkey	29.3
11	Chile	29.1
12	Czech Republic	28.7
13	Lebanon	28.2
14	New Zealand	27.0
14	Slovenia	27.0
16	El Salvador	26.9
17	Malta	26.6
18	Panama	25.8
18	Antigua	25.8
20	Israel	25.5
21	Australia	25.1
21	Saint Vincent	25.1
23	Dominica	25.0
24	United Kingdom	24.9
24	Russia	24.9
26	Hungary	24.8

hugely populous nations such as China, India and Brazil follow suit. We can see prosperity lead to changing diets and a shift from eating cereals and grains to the consumption of more fats, sugar, oils and animal products.

Currently more than half of the world's 671 million people who are obese live in 10 countries – the US, China, India, Russia, Brazil, Mexico, Egypt, Germany, Pakistan and Indonesia, with the US home to 13% of the world's obese population. One in three American children are either obese or at risk of becoming so.

But this should no longer be labelled the American disease. Over the last 30 years, the problem has become most acute in the Middle East and North Africa, with more than 58% of adult men and 65% of adult women overweight or obese.

With progress and development, it seems, come processed foods. Dr Margaret Chan, the World Health Organization's director general, has put it as bluntly as you'll perhaps ever hear:

> '*Our children are getting fatter. … Parts of the world are quite literally eating themselves to death.*'

> '*… we see no good evidence that the prevalence of obesity and diet-related noncommunicable diseases is receding anywhere. Highly processed foods and beverages loaded with sugar are ubiquitous, convenient, and cheap. Childhood obesity is a growing problem with especially high costs.*'[74]

Analysis of children's height and weight shows that children's BMIs were pretty close to being stable for the first 80 years of the twentieth century before they suddenly began to rocket in the 1980s. It seems that a key reason for this change was that marketing techniques for food and soft drinks with a high fat, sugar or salt content became a whole lot more sophisticated – and especially those directed straight at children.

There's long been discussion about when the 'magic age' is when children's cognitive skills begin to know that advertising is a one-sided debate, designed to encourage consumption rather than to give a rounded picture. (There's a strong argument to say that many adults struggle to see where fact stops and ad fiction starts, given how super-sophisticated marketers have now become.)

So the 1980s saw the real birth of pester power marketing, with fast-food restaurant gimmicks, confectionery packaging and cereal branding, to name but a few, all being funnelled straight into young, impressionable minds. In fact, research has found that Quebec, which banned fast-food advertising to kids in electronic and print media for more than 30 years, has seen a 13% reduction in fast-food expenditures and an estimated 2 to 4 billion fewer calories consumed by children in the province as a result. While other parts of Canada have been experiencing the same explosion in childhood obesity seen in the USA, Quebec has the lowest childhood obesity rate in the country.[75]

The reverse is true across the US border. Obesity levels continue to rise among children at the same time that six- to 11-year-olds in America were found to have viewed more than 700 TV ads for breakfast cereals annually, with cereal companies spending $264 million to promote their child-targeted brands in a single year.[76]

It isn't that hard to see how this all works or the terrible effect it is having, but unlike other health issues, obesity, and especially obesity among our children, is a fiendishly complex issue. And it works hand in hand with the rise in processed and unhealthy foodstuffs to produce an environment in the developed and developing world with the perfect conditions for weight issues to proliferate.

Starting a movement

The battle against obesity has centred thus far on what we put in. Calorie intake, fat intake, carbohydrate intake, supplements, appetite suppressant pills and, of course, endless, countless diets; the list of industries and sectors that have sprung up (and prospered) around the obesity issue is astonishing.

But the figures show that virtually none of it has made a blind bit of difference; the epidemic continues to spread unabated.

So what's going on?

We have stopped moving, that's what.

The computerisation and mechanisation of our work and leisure time through the 1970s, 1980s and 1990s to the extent we see today mean that most of us are burning far fewer calories per day than ever before in human history – exactly at the point when we are taking more and more in. And it's worse for today's children. Notwithstanding the odd running app, the proliferation of gaming and the virtual world our children are born inhabiting are a recipe for lower and lower calorific burn.

Our genetic make-up doesn't offer much solace either. A research team from the Medical Research Council's Epidemiology Unit in Cambridge delved into genetic susceptibility by reviewing the DNA of more than 20,000 men and women, specifically focusing on certain genes known to raise the risk of obesity.

What they found was telling – simple physical activity, like walking the dog or gardening, dramatically reduced the impact where these genes were present. So what should we do as parents to insulate our children from the obesity threat?

A complex problem needs a complex solution.

The first bit is simple. More and more evidence is suggesting that our diet alone, while important, isn't where we'll really combat the frightening onslaught of obesity – it's our day-to-day activity levels that need to increase too, and increase quickly.

Instilling a love of being active, avoiding using physical activity or sport as a punishment, and, crucially, making sure our children see us being active too are all key parts of making that happen.

But the onus can't just be on us; governments can help. In the UK, an aggressive encouragement of companies to market less salty foods since 2003 has, according to findings in the *British Medical Journal*, been at least partly responsible for plummeting rates of heart attacks and stroke deaths. Likewise, in Denmark, a 15-month-long tax on saturated fat led to, guess what?, a reduction in saturated fat intake.

And that's in the home of bacon and pastries.

New York City has banned trans fats in its restaurants, and Iceland and Switzerland have constituted outright bans too. These things can be done, as can bringing in bans and regulations on marketing foods high in fat, sugar and salt directly to our children.

Just as the once prevalent practice of sticking a child up a chimney to clean out the soot seems bizarre and barbaric to the modern sensibility, so surely in time will the fact that we allow our children to be repeatedly exposed to advertisements for food that we know is doing them no good.

Publicly funded media campaigns to try to tackle the relentless onslaught of child obesity don't stand a chance against billions of pounds of commercial communications budget intent on putting products directly and repeatedly in the line of sight of the most vulnerable, impressionable and important group of people there is.

The truth is that no country on Planet Parent has found a way to really turn back this troubling tide so far. And in an ever shrinking world, the chances are that we will all have to work together to find our way out of the nightmare we've made.

A parent's perspective

Professor Greg Whyte – father and global physical activity expert, UK

As parents, the modern threat to our children's health is inactivity. The price to pay for affluence is an ever diminishing requirement to move. Our lives and those of our children have now evolved into a 'box culture' where we sit in our 'home box', travel in our 'car box' to school, sit in our 'school box', travel home in our 'car box' and sit/sleep in our 'house box'.

The result is a population of children who are predicted to be the first generation to live shorter lives than their parents. While obesity has been the target of media attention in recent years, it is inactivity that is central to our children's quality of life. The beneficial effects of exercise not only include a reduction in diseases like heart disease and cancer, but it also has a positive impact on our psychological well-being, reducing depression and improving self-esteem.

Inactivity has been termed a 'pandemic' as it affects multiple nations across the world including those countries that, paradoxically, reside at the top of the Olympic medal table, i.e. USA, Australia, UK and China. This disconnect between sporting success and activity is evidenced by the fact that more than half of children in the UK fail to reach the World Health Organization guidelines of 60 minutes per day of moderate-intensity physical activity.

Put simply, they don't play for 60 minutes each day!

In responding to this sedentary diseased state, governments around the world have invested limited sums of money in a plethora of initiatives to increase the activity of children. These initiatives include active transport promotion (walking/cycling to school); increased and ring-fenced funding for physical education and extra-curricular activities; and in-class and break-time physical activity promotion. Relying on government initiatives to solve this problem, however, is only part of the solution, particularly when only 50% of a child's activity is attached to school (in the holidays it is usually zero). It is the responsibility of parents to ensure that their children are active.

Not providing sufficient opportunities for children to be active to confer health benefits could be viewed as child neglect. Parents are role models to their children whose influence during the early, formative years will last a lifetime. Over 80% of obese children become obese adults, and the same is true of inactivity. As parents, it is our duty to ensure that we lead by example and provide an environment on activity if we are to ensure that our children enjoy a healthy life for as long as we do.

WORLDLY WISDOM - FOOD

Wet nursing, the act of enlisting someone else to breastfeed your baby, died out as a practice over a century ago. But in the US today, it's making a comeback.

Using animal milk to feed babies has been recorded as far back as 2000 BC.

Listed as 'glucose-fructose syrup', 'high fructose corn syrup' and 'HFCS', this mass-produced super-sweet substance is found in a huge array of food products worldwide and is increasingly suspected of playing a part in the global child obesity epidemic.

The French Society of Paediatrics recommends what it calls 'food diversification', where parents introduce a different vegetable to their child's diet every four days or so once they are weaning.

The French also disregard texture and concentrate on exposing babies to multiple tastes via pureed foods.

Currently, more than half of the world's 671 million people who are obese live in 10 countries – the US, China, India, Russia, Brazil, Mexico, Egypt, Germany, Pakistan and Indonesia.

The US alone is home to 13% of the world's obese population, with one in three American children either obese or at risk of becoming so.

5
Learning

Communication
Doing what comes naturally?

M is for mama

Language is a true wonder of our world.

No other form of communication – not bees dancing directions, not dogs barking orders, not even dolphins clicking away in the oceans – gets anywhere close to transferring so much information in such a short period of time as we do.

But perhaps what's even more remarkable is that our young learn, from a standing start, to mimic, explore, practise and finally learn enough actual working language to communicate to an astonishingly complex level in just three years.

The way children learn different and utterly diverse languages is surely unique. The tongue positioning alone required to form sounds by the speakers of one language can reduce others to gibbering, slathering fools, unable to get close to a particular word or even part of it. Some East African dialects that I have come across seem so alien to what my mouth is capable of producing that I often literally don't have the first clue about where to start to replicate them. My tongue and teeth momentarily attempt to interact in the way needed but fail at the first hurdle.

Likewise, I was once told by an Aboriginal tribal elder in northern Australia that the difference between one indigenous language and another on that vast landmass is often easily greater than the difference between, say, English and Chinese, so diverse and independently evolved were they.

And what about the Khoisan languages of southern Africa that have used clicks for longer than most other languages on the planet have even existed.

Surely, with such a bewildering array of dialects, creoles and accents in the world, babies, toddlers and infants must somehow carry a genetic predisposition to being able to learn the language of those around them?

A clue to the answer can be found in the fact that there is a word, and seemingly only one, spoken in a strikingly similar way in nearly every language on the planet.

That word is 'mama', and its universality is pretty extraordinary. With very few exceptions, in almost every language humanity has created, no matter what its origin or geographical spread, infants use a recognisable form of it.

No other word, no matter how ubiquitous the subject matter it describes or how often it is used, comes anywhere close – not sky, not sea, not no, not yes, not anything.

As if that weren't enough for this super-word, it also happens to be, more often than not, the first word spoken by babies everywhere.

Proof, if it were needed, that mama does indeed know best.

But things aren't quite as straightforward as they may first appear. On closer inspection there seems to be an ulterior and rather more pragmatic motive at play, one that revolves around the one thing babies crave more than anything else.

No, not their parents. Food.

Russian linguist Roman Jakobson found that the easiest vocalisations for a baby to make, no matter where on the planet they are, are open-mouth vowel sounds, and that they can be made from the first seconds of life in the form of cries.

As the newborns begin to experiment with producing other noises, they test out some of the easier consonant sounds, starting with those made with closed lips such as 'm' and 'p', often in that order.

The little babblers then summon up the energy to deliver their newfound 'mmmm', but they get very tired very quickly and soon relax back into the familiar and easiest open-mouth vowel 'ah' sound.

Mmmmm Ahhh.

And why do babies choose to make the 'm' for mama before any other sound? Not because they have already heard mummy's name mentioned and are desperate to repeat it, but rather, according to Jakobson, because 'm' is the easiest for a baby to make while its mouth is busy feeding – which is why, even as adults, we still associate 'mmm' with something we like the taste of.

They soon get to the 'p', but papa and mama aren't the names all babies choose for their doting parents; they are the first two sounds we hear from them and decide, rather grandly, that they must relate to us.

Whereas what they both actually mean is 'this food stuff is lovely' or something very close to that.

By being recreated generation after generation, the simplest of baby sounds have essentially, over time, come to have a profound influence on our most basic family words in languages found right around the world.

The truth is, there is no genetic code that leads a child to speak English or Mandarin or Portuguese. Language is learned, and generally all of us, no matter where we're born, start equally with the capacity to make around 40 sounds.

In fact, an Australian former opera singer, Priscilla Dunstan, has gone as far as to suggest that we actually arrive into the world with five universal words or sound reflexes that are used by infants to communicate what irks them. What's more, she says that if we listen very carefully, we can identify them.

'Neh' means I'm hungry, 'Owh' I'm sleepy, 'Heh' I'm experiencing discomfort, 'Eairh' I have wind in my nether regions and 'Eh' I need to be burped.

The millennia of mystery of what babies need when they are in full cry are solved in one giant gurgling leap. Except that there's next to no science to back it up.

What has been proved is that from birth up to the age of five, children develop language at a very rapid pace and that, in general, the stages of language development are universal among us all, no matter where we live or – extraordinarily, when you consider the diversity – what language it is that is being learned.

In her book the *The Articulate Mammal*,[77] the language expert Jean Aitchison has identified the development stages we all share as being roughly: crying as a newborn; cooing at six weeks; babbling at six months; displaying intonation patterns at eight months; one-word utterances at a year; two-word utterances at 18 months; word inflections at two years; questions (lots of them!) and negatives at two and a quarter years; rare or complex constructions at five years; and fully mature speech by the time they reach 10.

There's little variation in the pattern or system of development between languages, cultures and locations, and no one language displays traits of being more difficult than another for children to learn – the ease with which children acquire different languages by the same age tells us we are all essentially just programmed to speak. Even though the planet's children aren't formally taught language, its acquisition is generally seamless and forms part of the overall development of our young.

So, on a planet dripping with grinding inequality, it's uplifting to find something so fundamentally important and key to how you survive or thrive which is universally available to all of us no matter what our circumstances.

Except, of course, that this isn't the case at all.

Learning the lingo

We might well all be born with the same capacity for astonishing language learning, but the catalyst needed to ignite that innate potential is exposure to language and interaction with others.

Take the babbling stage, for instance. Beautiful beguiling baby babble is increasingly being understood as the essential precursor to proper speech. Scientists have noticed that babies all over the world babble in very similar ways until at differing points in the second year of life they begin to shape their sounds into the words of their native tongues. In order to make this transition from general noise makers to fledgling talkers, children have to hear real language from real people. Television doesn't do the job; it's the quality of interaction with the adults around them that is key.

Mastering a language in infancy happens so often that it appears to be simplicity itself, but it is based on active, repetitive and complex learning. No matter what our location or social status as parents, the moments when a mother coos and baby-talks over the crib and when a father listens intently to his three-year-old's breathless telling and retelling of the newly discovered genre of the 'knock knock' joke are the very moments when children are learning to speak our language.

There is, of course, huge variety when it comes to the quality of this primarily parental speech interaction. If you happen to spend your formative years growing up in a war zone, among the many hurdles put in front of you will be the lack of face time required to lay those crucial and lifelong language foundations.

It doesn't require that drastic a scenario, though. A report by the UK's National Literacy Trust entitled *Talk to Your Baby*[78] put forward a whole raft of issues that could be leading to a situation that it referred to as an 'increasing number of children suffering from communication difficulties'.

Is the increased use of dummies with their gobstopper effect to blame? Is it the fact that the majority of modern buggies see children facing away from the pusher, unlike big old-fashioned prams? Or maybe us parents have our faces increasingly buried in smartphones?

Does the modern lifestyle that many lead mean we expect children to pick up the ability to talk because there's so much noise around them – not realising that what they need isn't noise but direct, close interaction to be able to learn what they need directly from us?

The television consumption of the world's children also comes into the cross hairs too, of course, as this has fundamentally changed the way the young get much of their early language stimulation. We'll look at this world in more depth shortly, together with the app and the touchscreen epoch the planet currently finds itself being swept away by.

No one really knows the impact such things will have on language, but what is absolutely certain is that, after the age of five, it becomes much more difficult for most children to learn language and there is even strong evidence that children may never acquire a language at all if they have not been exposed to it in the right way before they reach the age of six or seven.

Whatever the factors changing the way the parent/child language-learning relationship works at home, the way language is taught at school, especially the issue of second languages, exposes major national and regional differences. Not just in technique and timing, but also in views on how important or otherwise it is to instil in our children the need to speak more than one language.

Babel babies

Although the majority of the world's schoolchildren are taught a second language at some point in their school career, there exists a divide of sorts between nations whose mother tongue is English and the rest.

While English may no longer be the most spoken language on the planet, it is by far the most widespread. Except for the most remote spots, wherever you go you'll find someone who can at worst have a good go at conversing and at best have a mastery of the language that puts native speakers to shame.

On the face of things, this phenomenon of 'World English' looks to be a distinct advantage to nations whose children learn it – but it is increasingly being seen as a burden in today's world.

The often unspoken attitude that held sway for decades in places like the UK was that, if we're lucky enough to be already speaking the world's most important language, why spend valuable learning time on mastering another? And this has led to a situation in which many English-speaking nations are now being left behind.

Globally, the language picture makes for interesting viewing. In the Asia-Pacific region, for instance, India's past sees English used for official communication and therefore a compulsory language to learn in the majority of schools. English is also the most-studied foreign language in Korea, Pakistan, Japan and Taiwan, while in China, English is now a required language beginning in third grade.

In the Middle East and North Africa, second languages are taught widely, although which ones often depends greatly on which former colonial power figures most dominantly in their history. In Algeria, Morocco and Tunisia, French is the most commonly studied language besides the native Arabic, while in Egypt, the United Arab Emirates, Kuwait and Oman, English is again the main player.

Age ranges vary, but the worldwide trend is definitely heading towards the younger the better. Singapore and Hong Kong both teach languages at six and Finland at age nine – which, as we'll see, is only two years after they have started any form of formal education.

On average, across the European Union, 73% of pupils enrolled in primary education learn English as a modern language, while in lower secondary education the figure is over 90%.

What's more, on average, children across Europe are learning foreign languages at a younger and younger age, with most now starting when they are between six and nine years old, and some even offering them at pre-school age – the German-speaking community in Belgium, for example, starts as young as three.

The EU has a formal objective, set back in 1992 by heads of state at a summit in Barcelona, which is to aim to teach children two languages in addition to their own mother tongue from a very early age. Labelled 'mother-tongue + 2', it was introduced not only with integration and communication in mind, but also as part of a drive to give future generations the tangible skills and extra employability that mastering another language brings.

The scheme has generally been successful, and, after English, the second most widely taught foreign language across Europe is usually German or French, often depending on historical and political links.

Up until very recently, things were very different in the UK. Teaching languages had been compulsory from the age of 11 in the UK for many years, but in 2002 the British government made them an optional choice at GCSE for all 14-year-olds, and consequently the numbers choosing to learn a second language plummeted.

By 2012 the number of A-level candidates for French and German had fallen by a disastrous 50% in 12 years. This in turn led to few people reading languages at university and then institutions themselves offering fewer and fewer language degrees – creating a lack of language teachers further down the line.

Catastrophe!

This imperfect storm is at last being addressed, with all children set to be taught a foreign language from the age of seven from 2014/15 onwards.

It's a similar story down under. Almost every nation that Australia and New Zealand count as close neighbours and key trading partners in the Asia-Pacific region are bilingual or even trilingual, and there is now a concerted centralised effort to reverse a decades-long attitude that being born into an English-speaking culture is nothing but a blessing and a reason not to need to learn another language.

With its melting pot heritage, the USA is one of the planet's most linguistically diverse nations; while English dominates, as a nation the US doesn't designate any single language as its official tongue. Against this backdrop, the learning of second languages isn't federally compulsory and varies hugely from state to state. Looking at the number of students enrolled in foreign language classes in colleges and universities, though, the most popular languages learned in the US are Spanish, French, German, American Sign Language, Italian, Japanese, Chinese, Latin, Russian and Arabic.

With technology galloping on at such a rate, will it really matter if our children learn a different language to the one they learn in infancy? Won't there be an app for it all? Or a thing you stick in your ear, *Star Trek*-like?

Or maybe we'll all just speak the same TXT-based Twitter language, every sentence abbreviated to 140 characters or less?

Whatever the future holds for the manner in which we communicate, learning a language matters all right because studies have shown that having a second language not only puts money in your pay packet and makes you more employable, it's also likely to seriously boost your brainpower.

Researchers from Northwestern University in the US reckon that bilingualism fine-tunes the mind, profoundly affecting the brain, and even changes how the nervous system responds.

So potent a force is learning and speaking a second language, in fact, that recent research in Canada and Edinburgh has shown that it can delay the onset of Alzheimer's by four years.

Of course, if clinging to the notion that other people will learn your language has been wrong these past 30 years, in the next 30 it looks like there will be an even more compelling case for all of us to teach our children how to converse in as many languages as they can manage.

With the rise and rise of the BRIC nations (Brazil, Russia, India and China) and the subsequent gargantuan shifts in the socio-economic politics of an ever shrinking planet, there's perhaps never been a more important time in modern human history for us as parents to ensure that our children see language as key to their futures and take a keen interest in how it is taught at home and at school.

Talking of which, who does school best on Planet Parent?

School
The clash of the classrooms

Scandinavia versus South East Asia

There's an ideological battle being fought over the way the world educates its children.

For the past decade, two polar opposite approaches from diverse ends of the social, cultural and often political spectrum have been having a ding-dong battle at the top of the plethora of international education league tables that now make regular headlines across the world.

Perhaps the most well respected of all these gauges, the tri-annual Programme for International Student Assessment (PISA) is run by the Paris-based Organisation for Economic Co-operation and Development (OECD) and surveys 15-year-olds in literacy, maths and science. For more than a decade now its very top spots have been monopolised by what can be loosely termed the Scandinavian and East Asian models.

The two countries that represent these two educational ideologies best – and, in fact, have traded places these past few years for the accolade of best education system on the planet – are Finland and South Korea. And they couldn't go about things more differently.

Finland

The Finnish model starts its children in school aged seven, a full three years later than many other systems. While time in the classroom is central to the way most nations teach, to the Finns it's about children being ready to learn and having the time and space to find their passion. To them, the notion of formalising education any sooner isn't only pointless but also counterproductive, making children bored and frustrated by the time they reach the age when they would naturally be wanting to expand their knowledge and learn in a school environment.

Even once they have eventually started school, the core attitude to why children are there is fundamentally different to how the rest of us have been programmed to see things. Finnish youngsters are encouraged, required even, to go outside to play and run about on frequent occasions all day long.

Play is interspersed with formal learning rather than the other way round, and being outside as much as or more than being in a classroom is seen as key – whatever the weather. To the Finns, as with their fellow Scandinavians, there's no such thing as the wrong weather, just the wrong clothes, and children of all ages don snowsuits and regularly play in temperatures into the minus double digits.

Another area where Finland's method differs from almost everywhere else is around testing. The world of education has got the testing bug in a big way, but not the Finns; they take a pretty dim view of almost all standardised testing before age 16. Rather, teachers are trained to assess children in classrooms using independent tests created themselves, and every child receives a report card at the end of each semester based on individualised grading by each teacher.

Every now and then the Ministry of Education tracks national progress by dipping its toe into the work of a few sample groups from a range of schools and ages. As for the performance of teachers and administrators, the same applies: if a teacher is poor, it is the principal's responsibility to spot it and deal with it – a system that does away with the need for an enormous centralised standards body that 'inspects' teachers and schools alike.

The difference in ideology continues in terms of the actual work pupils do in Finnish schools. While most other countries teach many more formal academic subjects than non-academic ones like art and music, the latter are seen in the Finnish system, together with the likes of home economics, as life skills and an absolutely essential part of the curriculum, not a soft target to be chipped away at to provide more time for maths and handwriting practice (more on that particular issue later).

Oh, and while they're at it, they discourage homework too.

This is a system that seriously swims against the global tide and one that has its origins in a desire not to necessarily achieve excellence but to breed equality and ability.

Decades ago, when the Finnish school system was badly in need of reform, the authorities put at the heart of the new educational world they wanted to create not competition but the notion that every single child should have exactly the same opportunity to learn, regardless of family background, income or geographic location. (This view is also borne out by the baby box we mentioned earlier, which every Finn gets at birth.)

Education was and still is seen as not a means to unearth star performers but to provide a level playing field for all at the beginning of people's lives. That way, the individual can really flourish in adulthood, based on solid and universal foundations.

It's this approach that has led to Finland's table-topping success as well as a relentless stream of foreign delegations these past few years visiting the country to try to capture the essence of the 'Finnish miracle'.

But it's not the only country that has become a 'must visit' for the world's chief educators. South Korea has fast become the structured, head-down ying to Finland's creative, laissez-faire yang.

South Korea

Much as the Finns typify and, to some extent, have perfected the Scandinavian education model, so South Korea has come to be seen as the gold standard of the East Asia approach. As you'd expect with an ethos based on competition, coming top of the tree – as Korea did in another global education review in 2014 – is no mean feat with neighbours Japan, Singapore and Hong Kong all snapping at their heels, all reinforcing the success of the system the region employs to teach its children.

And it is a system built on relentless hard work, testing and a rigorously narrow focus on the traditional academic subjects. It's far from unusual for secondary school children in South Korea to be up by 6a.m., at their desks by 7.30 and, after a long school day, off to study at private tutorial sessions until way past midnight. South Korean parents spend fortunes on these after-school tuition centres, called *hagwons*, of which there are thought to be more than 100,000, with three-quarters of children attending them.

The punishing schedule and chronic lack of sleep has led to a 'four versus five' rule among some hard-pressed kids – you'll make it to the college you want if you sleep only four hours a day, but not if you rest for five or more.

Whatever the debate around the toll it takes, though, the results have been undeniably stellar, and the rate of educational change attained by South Korea is nothing short of astonishing. In just two generations it has moved from mass illiteracy to being an economic powerhouse, with global super-brands such as Samsung, Hyundai, Daewoo and LG built on the sheer hard work of its people, especially its young people. But it has come at a heavy cost.

So who wins?

As well as being top of the OECD education tables, South Korea also has the highest suicide rate of industrialised nations, with the most common form of death for the under-forties being to take their own life.

Finland, on the other hand, together with its Scandinavian neighbours, is regularly to be found in the top 10 of many a happiness and well-being survey.

Is that the casting vote, then? If we want our children to grow up happy as well as smart, should we be scrapping tests, letting schools regulate themselves and making the curriculum a whole lot less rigid and a whole lot more creative?

It's not quite that simple.

What very rarely gets mentioned in this ideological tussle is that the decentralisation in Finland today came as the result of over 20 years of tightly monitored, centrally driven education reform. It was only after this top-down change that the country moved from having a poor education system to a good one.

To make this happen, the Finnish parliament passed laws in 1968 to create a new basic education system that was built around the development of a common comprehensive school system and a national curriculum that meant students were all held to the same rigorous standards. The whole thing was also to be evaluated by a central state inspectorate.

Doesn't sound quite so snuggly snowsuit and creative play now, does it? But that's what it took to build the foundations on which Finland's decentralised, innovative education system could be created – to allow great schools to evolve, they first had to actively create and mould good, solid ones.

What's more, in the latest PISA index, Finland actually dropped out of the top 10, prompting headline writers across the world to have a field day with variations of 'Are the glory days Finnished?'

The irony, of course, is that a system which consistently topped league tables did so by not buying into the league table culture. So now they aren't top of the pupil pops, they give a Scandinavian shrug. One senior Finnish education official put it rather nicely: 'Education policies here are always written to be "the best" or "the top of this or that", but we're not like that. We want to be better than the Swedes. That's enough for us.'

So, while we can pick lessons from both the Korean and Finnish systems, it feels like a stark choice between the two polar opposites for most of us who sit somewhere in the middle. But among the differences there is one common theme that the two share and that could help us all.

Both countries believe that all children deserve access to an excellent education. While they have very different ways of executing it, they also both share a passion for learning and a belief that if every child is educated, the entire society benefits. This results in a cultural respect for teachers which elevates education to levels that leave most societies and parents looking on in envy.

A is for Apple

The rise of the machines

There are certain aspects of growing up today that are all but unrecognisable to someone like me, careering towards 40 like a faulty freight train in desperate need of an oil.

There's always been a generational gulf in technological know-how, for instance, which saw my mum wowing her sceptical folks with the magical pressure cooker, able to prepare food at near light speed thanks to the mysterious properties of condensed steam.

Then I stole the edge when it came to the setting of the new-fangled video recorder, going through a mere 19-stage process to record three hours of pointless telly while accidentally overwriting something dad wanted to keep forever.

But it's the pace of change, the sheer width of this gulf, that is so unrecognisable now. Where I had a VHS to master, my kids seem to be only ever two apps away from patching into the Pentagon's servers and playing shoot 'em ups with real weapons.

Researchers in the US and Scotland have discovered the reason why children from around the world appear to master new technology so readily and easily compared with us parents – they are smarter and more creative than us.

Academics at the universities of California and Edinburgh put together a study that recruited more than 100 pre-schoolers and brought them into a lab to play. They had to figure out how to turn on a music box that could be activated by placing clay shapes either individually or in combination on top of the box. After being shown different series, they were asked to have a go themselves.[79]

All this at an age when conventional wisdom says they have a very loose understanding of cause and effect.

What they discovered was that not only were four-year-olds pretty darn good at the task, but after putting a group of adults through the same test, the youngsters beat them hands down.

The researchers put this surprising result down to the fact that children approach solving the problem in a very different way to adults.

Children everywhere think in a much more flexible and fluid way than we do, it seems, and they dare to explore what looks on the face of it a pretty unlikely answer. Our experience and insight counts against us as we rationalise ourselves away from the more creative, unlikely hypothesis.

I've had first-hand experience of this myself after travelling with an iPad to some incredibly remote and poor areas of the world. Children who've had no chance of ever seeing anything like it before took seconds to be in complete control of it. The notion that the same would have been true had I lugged a PC with Windows 98 on it halfway round the world will make anyone who used it guffaw at the memory of asking the little paper clip man exactly where the 8,000 words they had just written had disappeared to.

The difference is that touchscreen technology has been created with an interface that is as simple, intuitive and unmediated as possible – you touch what you want to interact with. Baby, toddler, pensioner, no matter where on earth you are, it's an instinct that is truly universal, which is why this technological advance is like no other in terms of the speed of its colonisation and the firmness of its grip.

Anyone who has witnessed a toddler make their way to a TV screen and expect it to swipe or look on bemused as a picture stuck to the fridge stubbornly refuses to play ball knows that something really extraordinary is happening.

But how are the world's educators responding and adapting to this technology and touchscreen revolution? And should the whole thing scare the inhabitants of Planet Parent witless?

Pen versus finger

I look back on the time I spent learning to write 'joined up' at school 30 years ago and, despite the fact that I make a living of sorts out of words, it seemed an utter waste of precious learning time even back then.

If the hour after hour in primary schools I would spend practising lead-in strokes I never ever use now had been directed towards learning a foreign language, I might be able to order a coffee on holiday without having to do the 'drinky drinky' hand sign.

And yet in most parts of the world the same is still true today, with hours and hours of classroom and homework time being poured into developing a skill that, with the best will in the world, is going to seem antiquated, quaint even, to today's children when they reach adulthood.

Supporters of cursive resist its loss because it's a long-held cultural tradition – but then so was using a six-year-old to clean your chimney.

There is evidence, though, to suggest that handwriting training helps small children develop hand–eye coordination, fine motor skills, and other brain and memory functions. Some supporters in the US have even suggested it can help children end up in careers that require hand precision, such as surgeons and painters.

They've obviously never watched a child play Temple Run.

There are also studies from Indiana University suggesting that writing by hand increases brain activity and memory of concepts. Psychologists at Princeton and UCLA also claim to have demonstrated that students who write out their notes on paper actually learn more.

Across three experiments, students took notes in a classroom setting and were then tested on their memory for factual detail, their conceptual understanding of the material, and their ability to synthesise and generalise the information. Half of the students were instructed to take notes with a laptop or other electronic device and the other half to write the notes out by hand. The latter showed a stronger conceptual understanding and application of the material than their tippy-tappy classmates.[80]

The academics explained the findings by postulating that, because writing by hand is slower and more cumbersome than typing, students are forced to listen, digest and summarise so that they can capture the essence of what is being told to them. Which feels a lot like saying that while driving a hundred miles is a lot quicker and less effort than walking it, the latter is preferable because you'll appreciate your destination all the more when you arrive.

If you are wondering why all this research into cursive writing is coming from America, there's a very good reason – almost every state in the US has all but phased it out of the curriculum.

It's a controversial decision that has created much online outrage. Arguments for keeping cursive are impassioned if sometimes a little flimsy. For instance, creating millions of people who are unable to decipher old written letters from their grandparents seems unlikely, as does leaving children unable to communicate should there ever be a long-term global power outage!

The dropping of cursive comes with the widespread adoption of the Common Core curriculum in the US. This seeks to teach skills that are 'robust and relevant to the real world, reflecting the knowledge and skills that our young people need for success in college and careers'.

In other words, we're no longer going to waste our children's time teaching them something that will become as relevant and important to them as calligraphy is to us.

Of course, what's often overlooked in this emotive debate is that it's the joined-up part of handwriting that is being seen as obsolete in the US (a technique that evolved only to add speed to the writing process, something the keyboard then took further). For many who do still write by hand, cursive has been dead for years anyway. When CNN asked people to share samples of their handwriting, of the 268 submissions they received, 149 (55%) were printed, 75 were in cursive, and 44 were a hybrid of the two.

It's a brave decision by the US and one that we will only be able to judge a success or otherwise in time. Maybe it will prove to have been a grave mistake, leaving a generation of adults stranded, unable to write flowing script in a world where technology has disappeared and pen and paper are once again king.

On the other hand, the rest of us may look back and kick ourselves that our children continued to spend so much of their precious schooling on something that bears all the hallmarks of a dying art.

Across the border in Canada, law makers in Ontario and Quebec have also recently followed America's lead on this. Since the genie of digital communications is never really going back in the bottle, on balance it really is beginning to feel like the writing is on the wall for cursive.

It just won't be joined up, that's all.

Technology at school

Of course, handwriting is the tip of a very large educational iceberg when it comes to the impact of the technological revolution we find ourselves in.

Historically, from the 'computer nerds' of Tokyo in the 1980s and the young text-mad Filipinos in the 1990s to Indonesia today – a country whose young citizens' gargantuan usage levels of Twitter and Facebook have comfortably earned it the title of the 'social media capital of the world' – the centre of gravity for emerging uses of new technologies by young people has often been in the East.

When what used to be called information and communications technologies (ICT) provision was being considered in schools across both developed and developing nations alike, the rationale was that the obvious place to start was with secondary school students. After all, older students wouldn't break the kit, their use would be more relevant to what they were studying, and better qualified secondary school teachers would be more likely to be able to use the things.

But now many parts of the world have completely turned that on its head, with Asia and Latin America in particular moving forward quickly to ensure that it's the younger the better when it comes to technology provision. One of the main drivers for this volte-face is that, as we've seen, touchscreen or gesture-based computing is far more relevant to young learners than typing-dependent applications often found on computers.

Add to that the effect of the 'pass back' phenomenon and it has become obvious that schools could – and probably should – get pupils interacting with touchscreen devices as soon as resources allow. The 'pass back' being the action parents across the planet will be all too familiar with – passing their iPhone or tablet to the back seat on a long journey in its role as electronic content-rich pacifier!

From a position of relative obscurity only a decade ago, touch-screening is now so ubiquitous that the rate of change we are experiencing is not to be underestimated. This is a time of extraordinary transformation.

Just five years ago, low-cost laptops for students was the name of the game, and a hardware race began to produce a cheap, low-spec but highly dependable computer that would be in every school bag on every continent.

It didn't last long.

Now, all the effort is being poured into large-scale initiatives to put tablets or simple e-books or browsers into the hands of potentially billions of students. Substantial projects in Russia, Peru, Portugal, Argentina and Thailand are all well under way, with perhaps the most impressive in Turkey, where plans to provide 10 million students with a tablet each are in full flow. In the US, BYOD or Bring Your Own Device schemes are becoming more popular and in sub-Saharan Africa it now looks certain that just as millions in poverty bypassed the landline era and went straight to mobile phones (and now use them to transfer money in a way that is way ahead of the developed world) so the PC and desktop will be skipped and the tablet will be the entry point to the worldwide web for millions.

So if great swathes of the planet are clamouring to give their schoolchildren tablets to learn from, there can't be any argument that our children's time on a tablet at home is time well spent too?

Or can there?

Sofa surfing

When rumour has it that Microsoft and Skype are working on an interface that simultaneously translates what you say in one language at your end of a video call into an entirely different one at the other, it's hard not to wonder in awe at the kind of world our children will live in.

Against this backdrop of inevitable, if unpredictable, technological advancement, many parents are confused, eaten up by guilt when they 'pass back' the iPad or see our children skilfully playing on a smartphone rather than reading a book.

And this worry and uncertainty aren't without their justifications.

Australian paediatricians have backed new guidance issued by the American Academy of Pediatrics, which urges parents to impose a 'curfew' for smartphones on the grounds that children are growing obese because they spend too much time sitting in front of screens.[81]

Studies show that, on average, children aged between two and 10 years spend just under an hour a day consuming what is termed educational screen media. What's key, though, is that this hour includes an average of 42 minutes a day of educational TV or DVDs. That's a huge chunk and shows that the dominant screen at home is still the big one in the corner of the room.

There's one major industrial nation that recommends that absolutely no TV is best for children under two and that those older should watch no more than one to two hours a day of quality programming at the very most.

Is it those Finns again with their progressive thinking, or the French, maybe, bucking yet another trend? No, it's the home of TV itself, the US of A.

And when you look at the statistics, you can see why a curb is advised. Data keepers Nielsen suggest that the average US household has 2.24 televisions, with the average child spending 1,680 minutes in front of them each week. What's more, over 70% of day-care centres were found to have the television on for at least part of the day too.

All of which adds up to the typical American child spending around 900 hours in school each year but watching 1,500 hours of television over the same period – during which time they view an estimated 20,000 30-second commercials.

As far as very young children are concerned, Nielsen estimates that American children between the ages of two and five years spend an average of 21.8 hours each week in front of the TV – that's approximately three hours each day, or a quarter of the time when they're awake.

But the US is far from alone in its continued love affair with the goggle box. While the datasets might not be as wide ranging, surveys show that countries as diverse as Thailand, Turkey, the Philippines, Indonesia, Brazil, the UK and Japan are all in a similar ballpark when it comes to general viewing time.[82]

If the content is vaguely educational, though, that's OK isn't it?

No, apparently not.

A US study by *The Journal of Pediatrics* carried out at the Center on Media and Child Health at Children's Hospital in Boston and Harvard University said that TV viewing is 'neither beneficial nor deleterious to child cognitive and language abilities' for children under two.

The University of Washington's Child Health Institute cites a connection between TV viewing and attention problems in the very young, and a study of more than 10,000 people carried out at University College London found that the risk of becoming an obese adult increased by 7% for every hour of TV watched at weekends at the age of five.

As if the message wasn't clear enough, academics from the University of Queensland in Australia have gone as far as to say that every hour spent watching television shortens the viewer's life by 22 minutes, adding that TV viewing time may be just as bad for us as lack of physical activity, being obese or smoking.

So what about time spent in front of the second screen? Is the same true of the increasing amount of time spent by our children in front of smartphones and tablets?

Keep taking the tablets?

The Common Sense report on media use by children aged up to eight in the US found that in 2013 as many children (7%) owned their own tablets as adults had done two years previously.[83] Given the huge rise each year in adult ownership of tablets across developed nations, it seems entirely reasonable to expect a similarly large leap in the number of children owning and using tablets year on year too.

But are parents who choose to limit or even deny access to tablets actually keeping from their children the kind of technological intelligence that will be the lifeblood of their future prospects? Or are they simply keeping them safe from an as-yet largely unidentified set of risks?

The BabyLab at Swinburne University in Melbourne set about finding out, using an infant cognitive neuroscience laboratory designed to discover what's going on inside tiny minds.

It's very early days, but Dr Jordy Kaufman, senior research fellow and the project's leader, suggests that it's wrong to presume that tablets and televisions will have the same effect purely because they have a screen in common.

> 'When scientists and paediatrician advocacy groups have talked about the danger of screen time for kids, they are lumping together all types of screen use. But most of the research is on TV. It seems misguided to assume that iPad apps are going to have the same effect. It all depends what you are using it for.'

And there's the rub. There's every chance that the next generation of apps won't just be better teaching aids than those on offer today, they could be more useful than the traditional toys that many parents would still feel more comfortable seeing their children playing with.

It's devilishly hard to kick the habit of several lifetimes and say an iPad is just as good as a book – or even better. But if new apps are capable of communicating back to parents about children's progress, strengths and weaknesses, then there's a very strong possibility that we will all keep on taking the tablets for a very long time indeed.

The question facing the world's parents today is do you gamble to try to give your child a grounding in what looks like the modus operandi of their futures, or do you stick with what is familiar?

Until more is learned, there's really only parental instinct to go on to arrive at the answer.

There is one other factor that's worth considering, though. *The New York Times* has run an article revealing that parents working at some of the best-known Silicon Valley tech companies are sending their kids to a computer-free elementary school in California.

The philosophy at the school is that technology interferes with creativity and young minds learn best through movement, hands-on tasks and human-to-human interaction – and, according to the paper, many high-ranking execs at some of the world's biggest technology companies agree.[84]

What about the man who brought us the iPad, Steve Jobs, he surely must have been open to his children using as much of his own handiwork as possible? *New York Times* reporter Nick Bilton asked Jobs: 'So your kids must love the iPad?'

His response was: 'They haven't used it. We limit how much technology our kids use at home.'[85]

....

A parent's perspective

Sanna – mother and teacher, Finland

The Finnish school system is based on nine years of free, compulsory education that is divided into primary education (seven to 12 years of age), or grades 1 to 6, and secondary education, grades 7 to 9 (13–16 years of age).

Because education is free, the students get their books, stationery and lunch free of charge too, and after 16 years of age you are able to continue to either various occupational schools or upper secondary school, which are all voluntary, with the majority of students continuing to further education after secondary school. There is also free, voluntary pre-school for six-year-olds that is considered part of the education system and that most children attend, where learning through play is the key idea that helps future pupils to get ready for school.

In comparison to many other systems, the pupils start school late, during the year they turn seven. During their first years at school, the school hours increase gradually, starting from approximately 20 hours a week in the first year to about 25 hours a week in year six. This way the child has an easy introduction to school life and the school is not considered too demanding or daunting. This usually gives the children a positive outlook on school and education in general.

Homework is given daily, but after school a child has time to play and do other things as well. On the other hand, the short school days cause problems for parents who work longer days. Therefore, schools provide after-school care for those first and second graders who need it.

In assessments, pupils are graded using numbers from 4 to 10 – 10 being the top grade, 4 a fail. Assessment is very much knowledge-based and those pupils who cannot obtain at least 5 on their subject exams or grades will not be able to pass their year and will be kept behind for another year. This way every pupil will have basic knowledge and skills in most subjects. However, the Finnish school system is very much geared up for helping those pupils with learning difficulties. Pupils with special educational needs will receive help from special education teachers and there are different levels of special education for different students. The key is to provide the necessary help immediately when the problems arise.

The Finnish school system does not have standardised exams until the matriculation examination at the age of 19. We do not *have single-sex schools or set classes. In some cases, for example in mathematics, we have more advanced lessons aimed at students who will continue to upper secondary school and foundation lessons for those who will continue to occupational school. Otherwise, most lessons are taught in mixed sets. As there is no streaming, pupils are less likely to know, or be concerned by, who is bright and who is not, and therefore the education system is more equal from the pupil's point of view.*

Education is considered very important in Finland and teachers are generally valued and appreciated.

WORLDLY WISDOM - LEARNING

The Finnish and South Korean education models are consistently voted the best in the world – despite being diametrically opposed to one another.

Finnish children start education at seven, three years later than in many systems, and they have regular play, much of it outdoors, woven into their school day.

South Korean kids adhere to a punishing schedule. The chronic lack of sleep has led to a 'four versus five' rule among some hard-pressed kids – you'll make it to the college you want if you sleep only four hours a day, but not if you rest for five or more.

As well as being top of the OECD education tables, South Korea also has the highest suicide rate of industrialised nations, with the most common form of death for the under-forties being to take their own life. Finland, on the other hand, together with its Scandinavian neighbours, is regularly to be found in the top 10 of many a happiness and well-being survey.

The writing looks like it's on the wall for cursive handwriting in the age of the touchscreen. The vast majority of US and Canadian schoolchildren now don't learn the 'joined-up' approach.

The argument for ditching it is that it's a criminal waste of learning time to continue to teach children a skill that will be as relevant to them in adulthood as calligraphy is to us.

The 'pass back', as it's called in the US, is an action parents across the planet will be all too familiar with – passing their iPhone or tablet to the back seat on a long journey in its role as electronic content-rich pacifier.

But what is the effect of all this screen time?

Where TV is concerned, Australian academics have suggested that, for every hour spent watching television, the viewer's life is shortened by 22 minutes!

As for children's use of tablets and smartphones, it's still early days and the jury is out – but consider this: when asked if his kids loved the iPad, Steve Jobs responded by saying, 'They haven't used it. We limit how much technology our kids use at home.'

6
The making of a mind

The praise paradox
The East/West split when it comes to resilience

Praise be

In the particular place on Planet Parent where I happen to find myself, praise is undoubtedly king.

Across much of the Western world, the modern trend is firmly in favour of the notion that positive affirmation, reaffirmation and then a bit more affirmation on top of that are vital to building confidence and self-belief in our young.

Without it, the argument goes, you are left with no self-esteem, cowering in the corner to avoid a barrage of criticism at every turn.

As ever, though, there is no parenting panacea. And it's hard to avoid the feeling, as you hand out compliment after compliment and laud dodgy drawings and assaults on piano keys for all your worth, that non-stop indiscriminate praise isn't always a good thing.

It all comes from the right place, of course, but what if the urge not to crush fledgling confidence actually leads to children so psychologically brittle that when the first honest appraisal comes their way they crumble? Is it right to feed them an early diet that makes them feel that the world is their oyster, only for them to find out later that they can't even afford a crabstick?

I'm often around children in parts of the world where, as far as material things are concerned, they have considerably less than my own. What regularly strikes me is just how resilient, resourceful and regenerative even the youngest of youngsters are when the situation dictates – even in environments that are incredibly tough to survive in, let alone thrive in.

No matter how utterly dire the circumstances in which they find themselves, there's barely a country on earth where you won't find children making do and using their imaginations or whatever they can find lying around to fashion into toys and play. They might be short on praise or encouragement, as the adults around them struggle with the effects of poverty, disease or disaster, but the appeal of the freedom brought by something like a kite, for instance, means the drive to make one out of old bags and twigs doesn't come because they will be praised for it, but rather because if they don't no one else will.

When I spent time in Tacloban, the Philippine city devastated by a super-typhoon in 2013, it was truly awe-inspiring to see children surrounded by so much death and destruction exuding so much strength and hope by filling the skies with kites made in exactly that way.

These were children who had been through an ordeal so terrifying it left many of them clinging to power lines and coconut tree palms as the 13 foot storm surge moved inland. Gusts of wind at speeds of 235mph caused huge devastation, killing 4,460 people and leaving 1.9 million homeless.

And yet the resilience of these children, despite their ordeal, was undeniable.

Away from the extremes, when it comes to parenting there also exists a fundamental philosophical day-to-day difference in the way in which parents in the West and East approach the issues of resilience and praise.

At the heart of the disparity is the fact that, for parents in the US, UK and much of Western Europe, respecting their children's individuality and encouraging them to focus on their own passions and interests are key. Supporting your children's choices rather than making them yourself is the order of the day.

To do this, an often almost exclusively positive, nurturing environment is deemed to be necessary because, without one, self-esteem and self-worth will be hit hard (these are concepts that have also become vital to how the West develops its children). Many Western parents feel a huge anxiety about the effects of their children feeling a failure at something. So, in order to avoid what is now seen as the debilitating and destructive force of failure, parents constantly try to reassure their children about how good they are, even if the actual evidence on the paper or the piano stool tell a very different story.

Is there a right and a wrong way to praise children, though?

American psychologists Jennifer Henderlong Corpus and Mark Lepper analysed more than 30 years of global studies on the effects of praise and found that it can be a powerful motivating force if you are sincere, specific and realistic and give it only for traits kids have the power to change. They also found that it is key to use praise to encourage youngsters to focus on mastering specific skills rather than being better than someone else.[86]

They also highlighted a subtle point that was subsequently borne out by an in-depth study: namely that unless you are careful about overpraising kids for achievements that come easily to them, or that they love doing, it can seriously backfire.

A study from Utrecht University in the Netherlands asked more than 700 parents and teachers how they would react to a hypothetical child with either low or high self-esteem after they'd drawn a picture or solved a problem. The results confirmed that the adults would bestow twice as much inflated praise on those with low confidence in the belief that their sense of self would be boosted by doing so – which follows much Western parental thinking.

In the second part of the experiment, 240 children aged between eight and 12 first completed a questionnaire measuring their self-esteem before drawing a copy of a famous painting, which they were told would be judged by a professional artist. Each child then received a note about their efforts either overpraising, praising or not praising it at all – as opposed to actually criticising it.

The children were then given a choice of images to copy again and told that one was easy to recreate but they would not learn much from it, while the other was more difficult and while they would almost certainly make mistakes they would be sure to learn a lot in the process.

The children with low self-esteem who initially received inflated praise – those who according to the 'praise boosts esteem' theory should have been awash with self-belief – were by far the most likely to choose the easier image.

What became apparent was that children with low self-esteem were more anxious about maintaining a high level of praise once they'd received it and were therefore less likely to progress into more difficult tasks in case the flow of fulsome praise should dry up.

No! That wasn't the idea at all! So, if children with low self-esteem attract more excessive praise, it will make them more risk averse when it comes to failure rather than more confident to try new things no matter what the outcome.

Tricky doesn't do it justice.

There seems to be a sweet spot somewhere between where appropriate praise ends and inflated praise begins that is about the size of a postage stamp. It also seems that parents have to ask themselves how hard their child was actually trying when he or she displayed this behaviour, while simultaneously paying close attention to what happens when praise is delivered, in case it's reinforcing low confidence rather than tackling it.

Positive reinforcement served with lashings of praise is the technique *du jour* for many parents in the US and UK when it comes to shaping the way their children learn to act and interact. Are there better ways to help produce confident and independent children?

Maybe we should ditch the whole thing and look east . . .

The ire of the tiger

There's something of a stereotype that has appeared in Western popular culture these last couple of decades around perceived pushy parenting from the East.

It's often the 'tiger mother' who comes in for the most attention, painted as the cold, callous driving force, pushing her offspring to achieve, always with a hint of vicarious living lingering around for good measure.

As with all stereotypes, amidst the exaggerated and maliciously twisted projection, there's fact.

Let's take China, for instance. Generalising about a parental population running into the many hundreds of millions is foolhardy in the extreme, but I had it explained to me while there that Chinese parents tend to believe that the best way to protect their children is by preparing them for the future. Parents allow their young to really see what they're capable of and ensure that they are equipped with the skills, habits and unshakable confidence that mean they can cope and can deliver what will be required of them as adults (which, of course, could well include passing on those selfsame traits to their own children).

All of which, on the face of it, is very similar to what you'd hear from a parent in the West too.

But the journey to get there isn't just different, crucially it doesn't even start from the same point either. While Western parents are concerned about their children's psyches and self-esteem, as we've seen, parents in Asia often aren't. They assume strength, not fragility – and, on top of that, differing foundations in academic excellence aren't linked with intelligence in the same way as in the West either. What a child does – not what they are born with or which family they are born into – is seen as what matters most.

That subtly alternative view allows the struggle of children to achieve and the often difficult process of learning, understanding and eventually acquiring a skill to be viewed in a completely different light. Rather than seeing struggle as an indicator that you're just not very clever, that your ability level is low, that you have no talent for something, as is often the case in many Western cultures, in Asia it is seen as an opportunity to achieve. Because nothing is seen as coming without struggle and hard work, the process itself isn't stigmatised, hidden away or masked by overpraise. Rather, it is embraced head-on, harnessed and used as a pathway to mastering something.

Put simply, struggle, which includes initial and even multiple failures along the way, is seen as a sign of progress rather than a signal to parents to wade in with praise or even to give up and move on to something that 'comes easier'.

What this means in practice is that in areas that are viewed as vital, like maths and science for instance, an initial inability to grasp, succeed and excel is ploughed through using a combination of hard work and determination, often supplied in copious amounts by parents as they refuse to let their beloved children give up on the task and themselves.

From the outside, especially for cultures that see struggle as an indicator of lack of aptitude, this can look cruel and pushy – which is how misunderstood stereotypes are born. Not that they work only one way, of course; there also exists a belief among some Asian parents that they are simply willing to put more tireless effort into not letting their children succumb to the struggle than their Western counterparts. The inference being that they put more in because they care more about what comes out.

Without unearthing and understanding the key differences that underpin the Eastern and Western approaches, it's easy to see how the two views are formed of each other's parenting approaches.

But which system is best? It's tempting to look at the empirical results from the East in terms of academic and technical excellence in many areas and draw the conclusion that, if it were possible, a wholesale change to the Eastern approach by parents in the West would be the smart move (depending on what you think 'smart' means, obviously).

But, of course, each philosophy and subsequent approach has its own strengths and weaknesses. While Westerners worry that their kids won't be able to compete against Asian children who excel in many areas, there's also a growing worry among Asian educators and parents that their kids are not creative, or rather that the system dampens down the individuality and otherness that are often the catalysts for true creative thought and expression – something that the West's model tends to afford more of to its young.[87]

As the planet continues to shrink, it's to be hoped that less focus will be put on the stereotypical notion of each other's styles and that parents from the East and West will learn and share from each other's traditional views on the making of a young mind. If and when that happens, we are going to have some seriously gifted, creative and happy children on our hands.

Cotton wool kids
Is parenting really a risky business?

A nursery story

My youngest son's nursery has a vice.

Not a dinner lady addicted to spread betting, or a hard-drinking headmistress. No. A real metal, steady as she goes, I've got a very good grip on things here, vice.

And hammers and saws to go with it too.

At three years old, when he walked through the door, our Louis was naturally and instinctively drawn to anything sharp or otherwise lethally dangerous, so this immediately became his favourite bit of kit. From his perspective, the possibilities were almost endless. There were arms to be crushed, fingers to be mangled and eyes to be poked – and he and I both knew that, because it was in the nursery, it was all legit and above board and there was absolutely nothing I could do about it.

Despite my worries, it was also what sold the place to me too. Any group of staff courageous enough to install something so obviously dangerous in today's litigious, risk-averse world of childcare, not to mention being patient enough to fill in the three-quarters of a million forms and assessments it must take to get the nod for it, gets my vote of confidence.

Planet Parent is, of course, littered with societies and cultures whose children are given huge freedoms and responsibility at tender ages and respond by showing they are capable of astounding things. There are the Ache children of Paraguay, who by the age of eight display jaw-dropping orienteering and trail-finding skills in dense rain forests. Then there's the Zapotec youngsters in Mexico, who can recall the names of more local flowers than seems humanly possible. Or the many child shepherds I've come across in Tibet and many parts of Africa – unfeasibly young children tending to huge herds of big animals across vast tracts of often inhospitable terrain.

But in the industrialised world of today, finding a vice and a hammer among the usual sea of plastic wipe-clean nursery equipment is a real rarity. A mixture of regulation fuelled by fear has seemingly led to an epidemic of mollycoddling, not just at school but at home too.

At least if you believe the headlines.

In the US, 'hover parenting', as it's been coined, where children are constantly monitored by fretting parents, has long been a phenomenon worthy of debate and – with not a little irony – worry in its own right.

Ellen Hansen Sandseter, a Norwegian researcher at Queen Maud University College in Trondheim, has found that a more relaxed approach to risk taking and safety actually keeps our children safer by honing their judgement about what they're capable of. Children are drawn to the things we parents fear: high places, water, wandering far away, dangerous sharp tools, the lot. Obviously, our instinct is to keep them safe by childproofing their lives, but the most important safety protection you can give a child, Sandseter suggests, is to let them take risks.

Further Norwegian research has also found that a more relaxed approach to risk taking leads to fewer accidents not more, because it enables children to develop their skills in doing things that carry risk.

Which is blindingly obvious, of course, and becomes even more so when you apply it to other less risky activities like sport or maths. Continually keeping children away from something because they might not do it properly, then exposing them to it cold when they are older, would rightly be seen as a recipe for disaster and failure in almost every other avenue of parenting. It's because the stakes are perceived to be so high where safety is concerned that we often end up neutering any and every danger we see.

Getting a sum wrong is one thing, not knowing how to cross a road properly is quite another.

A favourite example of those in the 'things aren't how they used to be' camp is climbing a tree, which was once a staple pastime of many a child in the UK. If you saw a youngster up a decent-sized ash or oak now, the chances are the fire brigade wouldn't be far away.

Some of our European neighbours have managed to stem this tide of risk removal, though without falling into the reactionary 'health and safety gone mad' trap of blindly rejecting every advance in child safety. And without feeling that every measure is an attack on the values of the 'good old days', when a toddler falling from a poorly secured third-floor window was merely character building and seeing your son or daughter being launched through the windscreen of a seat beltless car was a price worth paying for the right to drive unfettered if you so wished.

Of course, there's certainly a balance to be struck, and countries like Germany and especially Sweden seem to have made a very good fist of doing just that. It's not unusual for five-year-olds in German forest kindergartens to be happily whittling a stick using a proper penknife, or for three- and four-year-olds in Sweden to cycle down quiet streets on their own or clamber on top of playhouses without a chorus of disapproval and panic raining down on them.

And yet they don't see child accident rates rocketing. Quite the reverse, in fact.

Accidents waiting to happen?

A major Unicef report, the only one of its kind, gathered masses of data to compile the cheerily entitled Child Injury Death League and to look into the unintentional deaths through injury of children in the world's richest nations. They found that Sweden was in fact the safest place for children in terms of accidents, lending weight to the initially counterintuitive thinking that giving our young the chance to encounter risk makes them less likely to come to harm rather than more.[88]

The report also unearthed a wealth of detail about what the risk to our children actually looked like. It discovered that injury is the principal cause of child death in all developed nations, accounting for almost 40% of deaths in the age group one to 14, and that, when aggregated, traffic accidents, drowning, falls, fires, poisonings and other accidents killed more than 20,000 children every year in the OECD nations.

Boys were also found to be an incredible 70% more likely to die by injury than girls globally.

While Sweden, the UK, Italy and the Netherlands occupy the top four places in the league table, at the bottom languish the United States and Portugal, where the rate of child injury deaths was more than twice the level of the leading countries, and below them Mexico and South Korea, where it was three to four times higher.

Although the research showed that the major types of fatal injuries were the same worldwide, trends did vary widely between countries, even within each specific accident type. For instance, children killed in road accidents are most likely to be car passengers in the USA, Turkey and Australia, pedestrians in Britain, Switzerland and South Korea, and cyclists in the Netherlands.

It's no wonder that we daren't let them out of our sight with a barrage of statistics like that to digest – and despite being compiled more than a decade ago, this influential report and the headlines it generated continue to reverberate around many of the world's richest nations. Taken at face value it's enough to make us all cower in the cupboard under the stairs – taking care to avoid colliding with the ironing board, of course.

But what the report also showed was that the likelihood of a child dying from intentional or unintentional injury isn't just small, it's becoming smaller.

For a child born in the developed world, the chances of death by injury before the age of 15 are approximately one in 750 – less than half the rate of 30 years ago. Even on the roads of the industrialised world, which remain the biggest cause of unintentional child deaths, the rates have been declining steadily for decades.

Individual nations have led the way in showing that collective social efforts rather than merely parental paranoia can significantly tackle child deaths. For example, the Swedes (again) initiated Vision Zero in a bid to reduce the number of road traffic fatalities on their roads to zero. It's an ambitious aim for sure, but a combination of safer crossings, pedestrian bridges, diverting traffic away from residential areas and schools and stricter policing has seen road deaths of children under seven plummet – in 2012 only one was killed, compared with 58 in 1970.

Canada did something breathtakingly simple too, which also made a huge difference. It gathered detailed data on each and every accident that happened over a period of time and addressed the causes.

Told you it was simple.

A huge range of issues were tackled as a result, from new bicycle helmet laws to safer playground equipment, from the impact of huge SUVs in collisions to trampolines, diving boards, the works. Canada even became the first country to ban baby walkers after it found that children were disproportionately hurt or killed in them. They didn't muck about either; if you are found to have one, you can be fined up to $100,000 or sentenced to up to six months in jail!

Way back in the 1970s, New York launched a Children Can't Fly campaign, which was as simple as insisting that window guards were installed across the city. Deaths from window falls declined by 50% in next to no time.

The decline of crime

OK then, never mind accidents, what about the bogey man, the world is bad and getting badder – quick, kids, into the cupboard.

The thing is, despite the ever rolling 24-hour news coverage and the ability of social media to inform us about almost everything that is happening to almost every inhabitant on the planet and almost before it happens to them, we are in the middle of a gargantuan global drop in all types of crime.

Why and how remain something of a mystery, but there is a smoking – or rather non-smoking – gun in the shape of a car exhaust pipe.

Working away in his laboratory in 1921, American engineer and chemist Thomas Midgley created tetraethyl lead to make new-fangled car engines more efficient.

For most of the century that followed, crime rose and rose in industrialised nations with leaded petrol-powered cars on their roads in big numbers. Then, about 20 years ago, lead started to be taken out of fuel. And guess what? The trend reversed – and every broad measure of crime you care to mention has been declining ever since.

Coincidence? Increasingly, social scientists think not. Where nations have brought in totally different crime policies, diametrically opposed in some cases to those of their near neighbours, it's not made a blind bit of difference – offending has fallen at a similar rate regardless. If you live in a country that has a higher than average crime rate, it's fallen. Live somewhere with a lower than average rate and it's dropped too – what's consistent is that if you had lots of lead in your atmosphere and now you don't, people are committing fewer crimes.

When you consider that by the 1970s studies were showing that children could be poisoned even by chewing fingernails harbouring tiny flecks of old leaded paint from their homes and schools, it perhaps should not be that surprising that millions of cars spewing out the stuff across the planet would have an adverse effect beyond creating smog.

So even though it may feel like we are living in a world that's more dangerous for our children, and even though it feels like the best thing to do is watch them like a hawk and never allow them out of our sight, it's probably not needed. And when you consider what 'hover parenting' can lead to in the long term, it's not for the best either.

What's more, Dr Peter Gray, a professor at Boston College in the US and author of *Free To Learn*, has posited that unless we as parents re-learn the habit of leaving children to their own devices, undirected by adults to play and imagine and interact and learn with each other, we run the risk of creating a planet populated by rampant narcissists.

Playing with others, without an adult intervening at every turn, is the primary means by which children build up their capacity for empathy. To play with others on a level playing field is to learn how to accommodate and behave in ways that reduce the chance of the other person taking their ball and going home. As Dr Gray puts it: 'To play with other children you must please them as well as yourself, and that means that you have to get into the others' heads and figure out what they like and don't like.'

If our children are denied this vital learning curve by us parents being around to mitigate and smooth things over on their behalf, often before situations have even arisen, they will miss out on a core skill – and this may render them incapable of getting on with others, let alone forming deep, meaningful, lasting relationships.

So perhaps it's not the open window or stranger danger we need to fear the most, but the play date – that construct of modern parental paranoia that turns children getting together to play into a social happening where the parents are actually the key protagonists, always there, always watching, rather than the kids.

Perhaps if we learn to kick the risk habit, we'll see once more that the kids are all right.

Discipline
What's 'wait till your father gets home' in Mandarin?

From the spank to the naughty step

I found myself wondering the other day how we would have coped in our house without the naughty step these past few years. It's a relatively recent invention brought about by the internationally successful *Supernanny* franchise and has become the discipline method of choice for millions of parents at lightning speed.

It's a simple rebrand of an old concept, of course, with exclusion being at its core rather than some innate fear of staircases themselves.

It goes without saying that its very existence wouldn't have been necessary across much of Planet Parent 30 odd years ago because there was another discipline method that had predominated for a very long time indeed – the hand.

Whacking our young might have fallen out of favour relatively recently in certain cultures and societies (although, as we will see, it is still very much alive and well), but its story goes back a long way into human history.

From Egypt to China, ancient India to Athens, pre-European America to Rome, it seems that children were hit and hit often – especially during their formal schooling. Oral and then written traditions show that corporal punishment was found on every continent and often intertwined into religion, with proverbs such as 'Foolishness is bound up in the heart of a child. But the rod of correction shall drive it far from him', which is to be found in the Old Testament book of Proverbs and had a deep effect for many centuries.

By the Middle Ages, teachers were almost always depicted with rods in their hands and a good thrashing at school was part and parcel of a boy's or girl's life. Then, in 1693, English philosopher John Locke wrote 'Some Thoughts Concerning Education' and explicitly criticised the role that corporal punishment played in education. The work became highly influential across Europe and may well have influenced Poland to become the very first nation to ban corporal punishment from schools in 1783 – a startlingly progressive move by the Poles that began the slow trickle of bans on corporal punishment in schools which continues today.

One of the main arguments often put forward to keep the cane, strap or slipper being wielded at school is its swiftness, with supporters pointing to the fact that as soon as the student has been punished he or she can go back to class and continue learning, with the added bonus that staff time that would otherwise have been devoted to supervising detention classes is not wasted.

Spurious? I couldn't possibly say, but the arguments against corporal punishment in schools are rather more wide-ranging and some might say weighty, no matter what environment it's administered in.

Numerous studies have linked corporal punishment to adverse physical, psychological and educational issues including aggressive and disruptive behaviour in class, vandalism, depression, attention deficit, poor school achievement, low self-esteem, anxiety and suicide.

But what about at home? Although there's little formal documentation, it's believed that throughout history children were hit at home just as much as they were at school.

It took until 1979, when Sweden outlawed the use of corporal punishment at home as well as in school, for the move to begin towards outright bans. As of December 2014, a total of 44 nations had made any form of corporal punishment illegal anywhere.

States with full abolition[89]

Country	Year	Country	Year
Estonia	2014	Venezuela	2007
Nicaragua	2014	Uruguay	2007
San Marino	2014	Portugal	2007
Argentina	2014	New Zealand	2007
Bolivia	2014	Netherlands	2007
Brazil	2014	Greece	2006
Malta	2014	Hungary	2005
Honduras	2013	Romania	2004
Cabo Verde	2013	Ukraine	2004
TFYR Macedonia	2013	Iceland	2003
South Sudan	2011	Turkmenistan	2002
Albania	2010	Germany	2000
Congo, Republic of	2010	Israel	2000
Kenya	2010	Bulgaria	2000
Tunisia	2010	Croatia	1999
Poland	2010	Latvia	1998
Liechtenstein	2008	Denmark	1997
Luxembourg	2008	Cyprus	1994
Republic of Moldova	2008	Austria	1989
Costa Rica	2008	Norway	1987
Togo	2007	Finland	1983
Spain	2007	Sweden	1979

Elsewhere, though, using violence as a means of disciplining children is still very much in vogue.

In the United States, while there are partial bans in place depending on either location or the age of the child, hitting children is still legal in the home across all states. It's outlawed in the public schools of 31 states and the District of Columbia, while two states, Iowa and New Jersey, extend their bans to private schools as well.

In practice, corporal punishment remains fairly widespread in American schools and homes, a fact for which a 1977 Supreme Court ruling, Ingraham v. Wright, is in part responsible. The case centred on James Ingraham, a 14-year-old student in Florida, who allegedly disobeyed a teacher's order to leave the school stage. Ingraham was held down and spanked more than 20 times with a paddle and was bedridden for days.

Ingraham's parents sued the school for violating the 8th Amendment, which prohibits 'cruel and unusual punishment', and for denying his basic right of 'due process'. But the justices upheld school beatings as constitutional.

Across the border in Canada, spanking by parents is legal as long as the child is not under two years or over 12 years of age, and no implement other than an open, bare hand is used.

In the UK, while school punishments are outlawed, spanking or smacking by parents is still legal, but it must not leave a mark on the body.

France is a particularly fascinating nation when it comes to this issue. As well as it being legal to hit your children at home, corporal punishment at school is also still practised – it's officially banned but not actually illegal.

The Fondation pour l'Enfance (Foundation for Childhood) claims that in three out of every four French families, parents resort at some point to smacking or slapping their children. This picture of prevalence was backed up in a study that interviewed 1,000 French parents about their use of and attitude towards corporal punishment. More than 70% said they had 'mildly' slapped their child on the face and 87% on the bottom; 32% had given their child a 'resounding' slap on the face; 4.5% had beaten their child with an object; and just 7.9% said they had never used corporal punishment.[90]

Not only did a further survey of children by the Paris-based Union des Familles en Europe find that 95% of respondents had been smacked, it also revealed that more than two-thirds of the children said that smacking was a regular part of their lives, with over half even believing that they deserved it.

Could this be the reason why they don't throw food perhaps?

It never did me any harm

Elizabeth Gershoff, a developmental psychologist at the University of Texas who specialises in studying how discipline affects children's development, carried out an extensive review of the most recent research into the spanking of children.

In a paper entitled 'Spanking and child development: we know enough now to stop hitting our children', she concluded that spanking destroys mental health, increases delinquency and criminal behaviour and makes it more likely that the child will be physically abused. She also looked into the differences that ethnicity or culture make to those outcomes.

There were none.

Essentially, wherever you are on Planet Parent, whatever your cultural, historical or family background, the study found that spanking increases aggression in any child, anywhere.[91]

No amount of research will stop corporal punishment from being part of millions of children's lives overnight, but as it slowly dies out from country to country, what else is out there in terms of techniques and philosophies to discipline children? Is the naughty step or the threat of other unwanted consequences all we've got to call upon as our walls are covered in crayon and the cat is, in a very literal sense, rubbed up the wrong way?

In China, discipline is based on ancient Confucian ethics and the belief that infants arrive from the gods with an inherently good nature that is to be respected. This concept fosters interdependence within families, requiring that the elders responsibly teach, train, educate, discipline and govern the kids.

Many of the elder generation in the UK would recognise that joint responsibility approach, encapsulated in the 'it takes a village' concept. There was a time in Britain when everyone felt that they had the right – the duty indeed – to keep other people's kids on the straight and narrow (often with a clip round the ear, it has to be said). There's no doubt this broad notion of collective nurturing, of keeping an eye out, has been widely lost by the urbanites of the UK, although it very much exists elsewhere in the world, especially in rural communities.

In Japanese culture, Shinto beliefs traditionally regarded children under seven as belonging to the gods. And in order to keep those gods happy, young children were indulged and treated with leniency so that they did not decide to return to the heavens.

This belief system still lingers in modern Japanese parenting. Mothers, who are often responsible for disciplining children, rarely display anger and an emphasis is placed on explaining the consequences of children's actions.

Moving on from these ancient philosophies, there's also a new game in town – and it's questioning if even the naughty step is, well, a step too far.

Termed 'positive discipline', it's fast becoming a grass-roots hit with parents opposed to hitting in the USA and Australia and aims to teach children self-control and empathy, while adults are encouraged to think harder about the causes of bad behaviour rather than merely reacting to it.

Negative timeouts like the naughty step are frowned upon on the grounds that making children act better in the long term by making them feel worse is plain daft – the Australian Association for Infant Mental Health has even gone as far as to say that the approach is inappropriate for children under three as children of that age can't assimilate their own emotions, rendering the experience pointless at best.

Bribes (such a harsh word – rewards maybe) are out too as they could well prevent children from feeling genuine pride in a job well done, rather than just material gain.

Instead of banishing kids to their room, this new system advocates 'positive discipline', which means asking children to go to a 'calm-down corner' to regain control. Crucially, parents may need to do this too if they've been wound up to a point where they've stopped thinking clearly – something that all of us know is occasionally very possible indeed.

When all is a picture of calm, both sides can then work out how to fix the issue at hand.

If that doesn't work, then you simply join the kids on the naughty step and set up home there.

The entire debate around the disciplining and especially the corporal punishment of children is as divisive a parental issue as you'll find – the global success of the Australian novel *The Slap* is a testament to just how much it stirs up a stink.

Perhaps the last word on it for now should go to Tony Little, the current headmaster of Eton College, a school so historically synonymous with the beating of its pupils that it used to officially set aside Friday as 'Flogging Day'. Talking to the *Daily Telegraph*, the man who in previous generations would have been considered the UK's beater in chief had this to say:

'As someone who's been a headmaster for 20 years, I have never felt corporal punishment can be useful as a deterrent, or as a way to convey a message. It's a very redundant approach.

There's been a generational shift. It's just so far off the radar from being considered now. We teach boys through their life and work to respect others.

Laying into someone physically is just not appropriate.'[92]

....

A parent's perspective

Anne-Cecile – France

French kids are apparently known for 'not throwing their food everywhere' but that's because food is so important in the French culture that you don't play with it, full stop!

Discipline in a typical French household starts around the table. Family meals remain a must and kids are expected to sit properly, behave, have both hands on the table (never their elbows!), use their fork or spoon and eat what is on their plate or wait for the next meal.

Despite some changes towards a more lenient education after 1968 (when our mums and dads took to the streets to protest against the traditional society), a lot of French parents still believe that putting boundaries and having rules in place early on is best for everybody and it's never too early to learn how to behave and how to control yourself.

The school system is also more formal than what I can see from my time living in England . . . with less space left for self-expression and creativity and more for maths and structured learning.

How we discipline our children is actually quite similar to what I've seen in the UK: naughty chair or timeout (which we call 'aller au coin') is common practice, as are the usual threats or punishments (no TV for a week, taking away a favourite toy, no bedtime story or no play date . . .). Maybe the difference is that we actually mean it and our kids know it (the threat becomes reality quickly and often enough for them to take it seriously).

Corporal punishment, which was quite commonplace when I was a child, is no longer as widespread in French society and only a few very traditional people would use it as a common way to discipline their children. However, the odd slap on the bum doesn't seem to be perceived as badly as it is in the UK, and although I don't personally use it, it remains the supreme threat.

WORLDLY WISDOM - THE MAKING OF A MIND

When psychologists analysed more than 30 years of global studies on the effects of praise on children, they found it can be a powerful motivating force – but it must be used in the right way.

The advice is to be sincere, specific and realistic when you give praise and only give it in relation to traits or activities that kids have the power to change. It's also vital to use praise only to encourage youngsters to focus on mastering a specific skill, rather than being better than someone else.

There is a real balance to be struck, though. It has been found that overpraising children for achievements that come easily to them, or that they simply love doing, can backfire. Also, if children with low self-esteem are overpraised, it can breed a fear of failure rather than confidence.

At the heart of the difference between the way children learn and develop in East and West is a subtle but vital point.

In the West, struggle is often seen as an indicator that you're just not very good at something.

In many Asian cultures it is seen as an opportunity to strive and achieve. Nothing is seen as coming without hard work, and the process of struggle itself isn't stigmatised or hidden away, but rather embraced, harnessed and viewed as an essential pathway in mastering something.

Norwegian research has found that a more relaxed parental approach to risk taking and safety actually keeps our children safer and leads to fewer accidents, not more. Children's judgement and knowledge of self are boosted by risk taking and they develop their skills more by doing things that carry risk, which in turn keeps them safer.

A major Unicef report found that Sweden was the safest place for children in terms of accidents. At the bottom of the table was the United States and Portugal, where the rate of child injury deaths was more than twice the level of the leading countries, and below them Mexico and South Korea, where it was three to four times higher.

Poland was the very first nation to ban corporal punishment from schools in 1783. It took until 1979, though, when Sweden outlawed the use of corporal punishment at home as well as in school, to start the move towards outright bans. Today, a total of 44 nations have made any form of corporal punishment illegal anywhere.

In the United States, while there are partial bans in place depending on either location or the age of the children, hitting children is still legal in the home across all states.

7
The
finishing
touches

Modern parents
Are all things really equal?

For millions of people, at the very heart of this question is the battle between parenthood (particularly motherhood) and the need to work.

On the one hand it's easy to imagine that the difficulties of combining work and motherhood are relatively new, that going back to work after having a baby is a recent phenomenon. But it has happened for centuries, of course, and continues in much the same way in countless communities across the planet that still use subsistence farming as the primary way to feed themselves.

Many of the Tamang women of Nepal, for instance, return to work a week or two after giving birth and carry their new-born baby in a basket while they tend to crops and animals. A shortage of labour means they have to get back at it straight away and the only option for childcare is to leave the baby at home with an older sibling. As soon as children are old enough to help in the fields, though, that's exactly what they do, so it's either having very young children looking after babies or carrying them yourself while you toil all day. This picture of motherhood is one replicated in many parts of the planet, given that more than a billion people globally still live on less than $1.25 a day.[93]

While the world's industrialised economies are relatively awash with cash, there has been a systemic parenting problem of a different kind brewing over the past few decades. The issue starts with the fact that we are living longer and, as we've seen, tending to have fewer children. These two trends shrink the supply of skilled labour and reduce economic growth, and – so the economic theory goes – this soon begins to lower living standards in the developed world.

We're all doomed!

Never fear, though, mother is here. Or at least that's what long-term economic growth hinges on, business leaders and economic eggheads alike conclude.

No pressure then. Just rear the next generation and save the world's economy while you're at it.

I don't know how she does it

Babies and Bosses, a study by the Organisation for Economic Co-operation and Development (OECD), said that: 'In many industrialised economies, an increasing female (especially maternal) labour supply is seen as being important to maintaining economic growth and ensuring sustainable pension and social protection systems more generally.'[94]

The OECD's own figures for the percentage of women in employment in 2013 across the industrialised world show just how many are rising to the challenge (although not all are mothers, of course). The percentages range from 41% in Greece to over 70% in Denmark, the Netherlands, Norway, Switzerland and Sweden, with Iceland coming top at 78.5%.[95]

In fact, in several European countries, women with children are more likely to be employed than women without children. In the US, mothers are now the sole or primary income provider in a record 40% of households with children – that's nearly four times the rate in 1960.

But while the workforce might be approaching gender parity, it doesn't mean equality exists when it comes to work at home.

In the UK, by and large we live in an age of greater gender equality and certainly one in which men and women shoulder the burdens of home, family and putting bread on the table with something approaching equity.

A male friend of mine who considers himself (in conversation with me, anyway) to be pulling his domestic weight and then some was wondering out loud the other day if British men weren't the most hardworking at home of all of our brothers across the planet.

Which country, he asked, could possibly have a male population doing more to keep house, home and family running smoothly?

Well, there's Australia for starters.

The seemingly ever inquisitive OECD recently looked into 'the unpaid economy' of housework and childcare in 29 countries and who was doing it.

Contrary to the stereotypical image of the macho Aussie male, the research found that men down under spend 69 minutes a day looking after their offspring at home, compared with just 63 minutes a day for the men of Britain.

Fair dinkum.

That's nothing, though, compared with the great Danes, who came top of the tree and spend nearly three hours a day on unpaid work at home.

At the dog house end of proceedings, the men of South Korea brought up the rear with less than 50 minutes a day clocked up.

What's more telling than this league table of dad's dusting and dishwasher loading is that, despite the greater perceived gender equality in every single country the OECD looked at, women, working or not, still spent more of their day doing housework and caring for children than their men did. Norwegian women were found to spend just under four hours a day on unpaid childcare and housework, rising to six hours a day in India, Turkey, Portugal and Italy.

So, to recap, the future security of the global economy of most of the industrialised world, including pension funds, lies in the hands of the people who bear children and then do by far the most to look after and house them.

Childcare – you paid *how much*?

The very least these millions of superwomen deserve is affordable, accessible childcare. On that, the nations of the world can surely all agree?

Not so much, no.

Families in the UK, for instance, are shelling out more over the course of 12 months on part-time childcare than they are on mortgage payments. A Family and Childcare Trust report discovered that a family with one two-year-old child at nursery for 25 hours a week and a five-year-old at after-school club will be forced to cough up £7,549 a year on average to cover it all.[96]

This compares with an annual average mortgage cost in the UK of £7,207.

Now, I'm no socio-economic expert, but that doesn't seem at all sustainable to me. Childcare costs in Britain have seen a greater-than-inflation rise every single year since 2002. And they've increased so much that more than a quarter of UK salaries now goes towards looking after children – a greater percentage than in any other country aside from Switzerland.

Childcare across the OECD[97]

Country	Cost as % of net family income	Country	Cost as % of net family income
Switzerland	50.6	France	10.4
UK	26.6	Netherlands	10.1
Ireland	25.6	Denmark	8.9
USA	23.1	Korea	8.5
New Zealand	18.6	Finland	8.4
Canada	18.5	Czech Republic	6.6
Japan	16.9	Luxembourg	5.4
Australia	14.5	Iceland	5.0
Slovenia	13.7	Portugal	4.8
Austria	11.8	Poland	4.8
Germany	11.1	Spain	4.7
Israel	11.0	Belgium	4.7
Norway	10.8	Sweden	4.7

As ever, Sweden has taken a very different route to most other countries. Their super-well-funded social security system makes it not only easy to arrange affordable childcare but also ensures that parents can take regular time off work to be with their children too. A month of childcare will set you back the equivalent of just £110, and each Swedish child benefits from 480 days of combined paid parental leave.

Unsurprisingly it's a very popular system, but it comes at a cost and requires a cultural approach that one wonders will ever be fully embraced outside Scandinavia. Sweden is a country that has chosen to have the state spend more on pre-school childcare than on its defence budget.

Of course, with a population of not even 10 million and a parental benefit allowance costing around £3 billion a year, they pay eye-wateringly high taxes across the board to foot the bill for what often looks from a distance to be bordering on a social utopia. An approach they have thus far repeatedly voted for at the ballot box.

So if Sweden is notionally the best place to juggle modern parenthood, where's the worst?

Japan perhaps?

The Land of the Rising Sun has a triple whammy of a brutal working culture with hours and practices so prohibitive that around 70% of Japanese women still give up work as soon as they have their first child. Japanese men are then also far behind their counterparts elsewhere when it comes to helping out around the home and with childcare; studies have shown that Japan's fathers spend on average just 15 minutes a day with their children.

Then there is paternity leave. While Japanese men are entitled to take it, the pressure of the work culture actually means that only a tiny minority do – just 2.63% according to the Ministry of Health, Labour and Welfare.

Away from the extremes of Scandinavia and the tiger economies of the Far East, what happens to other couples in the modern world when they decide to plunge into parenting?

The baby bomb

The code of female conduct quite clearly forbids any member from frightening the maternity pants off another with graphic and gratuitous descriptions of contractions, forceps and stitches weeks before they are due to experience at least one or even all of them.

And quite right too.

What kind of world would we live in if it was socially acceptable to reduce pregnant women to emotional rubble with information that can only serve to haunt them as they approach their due date.

One without the human race, perhaps.

But there is another parental area where information is wilfully withheld, it seems, where the greater good is invoked, where the tough stuff is left out.

And it's the baby bomb. The explosive impact a 9lb bundle of joy can have on the modern relationship.

Everyone expects some level of change or disruption, of course they do – but nothing that can't be handled. How bad can a few broken nights' sleep be, after all?

The answer, as many parents reading this will know, is very bad indeed. Especially when you've both got work in the morning.

But we're not merely talking about lack of sleep here, or a dwindling bank balance – we're talking about the fundamentals of the very relationship that brought this baby into being in the first place.

A generation or two ago in most countries, the rules of engagement were pretty clear and had been for hundreds of years – dad at work, mum with baby. This clear but often unhappy post-Industrial Revolution arrangement has led to many a father missing out on their little ones growing up. As we know, though, this set-up has been changing in recent years, with many modern relationships now being built on a more shared model of responsibility.

As we've also seen, it's a long way off full parity. Mothers are still carrying a big chunk of the burden not only at home but at work too. But increasingly the pre-parenting expectation across much of the industrialised world is that having a child is a joint venture and demands as close to equality as you both can muster. After all, nowadays holidays are booked and cars are bought jointly – and as for cold hard cash, figures show that the number of households where the female is the major breadwinner is on the rise every year.

We increasingly live in a society where, at long last, the two genders of our troublesome little species are at least starting to live in something resembling equality.

Then along comes baby.

An evolutionary unit unchanged in thousands of years. It's hungry, it's here and it's not read much Germaine Greer.

Suddenly, for the lady of the house it's 1953. No matter how helpful her partner is and intends to be, for a good long while the rest of her life can go hang according to the insufferably beautiful but downright demanding dot in the cot.

While the running of the household – the cooking, the cleaning, the washing – may have been on a more equal footing pre-baby, there can often be an unspoken pressure for the mother at home all day to pick up the majority of that as well.

Unsettling, unnerving and seemingly never-ending as this feels to mum, it often has a knock-on effect on dad too, as the otherworldliness of the situation changes attitudes and temperaments. His efforts to help can be dismissed as pathetic, his pleas that a tough day at work means he is tired can be scoffed at, and his bewilderment about how to cope with not one but apparently two new people in his life can be absolute.

In truth, though, a new baby changes everything for both partners and requires a fundamental readjustment of how their relationship works, not just in the first few months and years, but for good.

What's required for them to adapt during this tumultuous period of change is patience, good humour and understanding on both sides – rare commodities indeed after three nights of no sleep.

And no one tells you! The other couples already in the family way never mention it, save for the odd coded comment or hidden smirk.

The swines.

But don't worry. Once the first gruelling few years are negotiated, happiness and joy break out.

Mmmm. It has to be said that there is a wide variety of academic research from many industrialised parts of Planet Parent showing that parents are not happier than their childless peers at any stage of the process. And in many cases they are considerably more miserable.

A key study by American Daniel Kahneman, a Nobel Prize-winning behavioural economist[98] who surveyed almost 1,000 Texan women, found that being with and taking care of their children ranked sixteenth in pleasurableness out of 19 activities. Cooking, watching TV, exercising, talking on the phone, napping, shopping and even housework were deemed to be preferable to spending time with the kids.

This same result shows up regularly in relationship research, with children more often than not reducing marital satisfaction.

Economist Andrew Oswald, who has compared tens of thousands of Britons with children with those without, broadly draws the conclusion that being a parent makes you neither happier nor unhappier than the childless. Unless you have more than one child, that is, which is when studies say you definitely start tipping into the unhappy camp!

The list of research goes on and on, with the US featuring heavily in the pursuit of parental unhappiness.

Have so many American parents always been this disaffected, disillusioned and, well, depressed? Probably not. In pre-industrial America, parents loved their children, of course, but their offspring also had a job of their own to do, a separate purpose from delivering bucketfuls of happiness to their parents. It was bucketfuls of potatoes instead, as they worked the farm and generally helped out in the household – much as they still do in many non-industrialised societies today.

Is this at the heart of why many residents of Planet Parent today report feeling so unfulfilled? Rather than having children out of the necessity for survival, today we have kids for emotional reasons and we expect that emotional payback to be relentlessly positive.

When our increasingly complicated, fragmented work and social world means expectation levels rise and satisfaction levels go south, things start to feel shaky.

A study by the University of Wisconsin–Madison carried out 20 years ago found that parenthood was perceived as being significantly more stressful in the 1970s than it was in the 1950s, with major shifts in employment patterns pointed to as the cause.

Jump forward to today, a world infinitely more complicated and fast-paced than the 1970s, where expectation levels have soared – especially where the concept of happiness is concerned – and it's easy to see where we've lost our way a little when it comes to what we believe being a parent should feel like all of the time.

Planet Grandparent
What's happened to nanny and granddad?

Granny knows best

Before we look at grandparents in today's world, it's worth recognising that they have played a vital but almost totally unheralded role in how parenting, and indeed our species, has evolved.

In fact, there's mounting evidence to suggest that if it wasn't for grandparents, we may have remained in the lower primate leagues when it comes to procreation and development.

Around 30,000 years ago, it seems the number of adult humans reaching the age of 30 started to rise dramatically and that soon afterwards there came a very substantial increase in almost everything – from artistic expression and food production to the making of tools and weapons.

Our brains essentially exploded into life, and, what's more, according to anthropologists at Central Michigan University, there is most definitely a connection between the surge in numbers of elderly humans and the cultural expansion that ultimately led to us becoming the species we are today.

That's right. Nana and granddad are responsible for us being masters of the entire planet.

No wonder they need a sit down.

When we started living to an older age, population sizes rose. And, after studying today's Hadza hunter-gatherers of Tanzania and observing that canny grandmothers who knew exactly how and where to forage led to healthy Hadza kids, scientists realised that was also exactly what enabled our ancestors to flourish.

Research suggests that while females would have normally died at child-bearing age, an occasional hardy woman would have lived a little longer and helped her daughters to dig and forage for food. As these grandmother/mother teams thrived, evolution did the rest and their genes were passed on to begin a slow but amazingly significant rise in the number of senior citizens.

It wasn't just granny power, though – good old granddads got in on the act in their own way too. A study of fossils from different parts of the planet and periods of human evolution found that few of our ancestors made it to the age of 30. But when researchers looked at Homo sapiens who evolved in Africa and migrated to Europe around 40,000 years ago, they found that adult survival rates began to rise at a point relatively late in human evolution.

Whatever the reasons behind this change, and no one really knows what they were, the effect was essentially the creation of elders who not only had a wider experience base, but stuck around long enough to pass it on to their children's children.

It wasn't just about knowing where the best water holes were either. Elders built relationships, resolved disputes and passed on wisdom.

In effect, what grandparents did was transform life from the short, brutal affair it had been into something resembling what we recognise today.

And they did all that by lending a hand with their grandkids!

Grandparents today

Fast forward to Planet Parent today and the role of the grandparent in the rearing of their children's children is hugely diverse depending on where you find yourself.

There are, of course, cultures where grandparents still play an absolutely key role within the family structure. In traditional Native American cultures, for instance, community elders and grandparents carry marked responsibility for the raising and especially the education of children. Areas such as cultural knowledge, spiritual awareness and kinship ties, which have been passed down for generations, are held dear and it's the elders who work hard to keep them alive in their modern, often city-dwelling grandchildren. Older women in particular hold a special status and are noted for their dedication to the cultural nourishment of their young family members.[99]

They also often request that their grandchildren stay with them for extended visits so they can soak up the Native American way of life. The archetypal atmosphere is one of the grandmother's firm guidance being complemented by the grandfather's gentle and affectionate approach.

Tammy Henderson, associate professor at the Department of Human Development and Family Sciences at Oklahoma State University, has said of Native American grandparents that they look to teach their young to 'do no harm, show respect, be quick to listen and slow to speak, and to give back to their community', which all sound like lessons well worth learning.

In Italy, there is a saying that sums up how the grandmother is a similarly central figure – 'When nothing is going well, call *nonna*.'

Unlike many cultures, where a grandparent's involvement in both their child's and grandchildren's lives decreases with age, Italian grandparents tend to provide significant help to their own children when it is time to raise the next generation of the family. Much of this support is possible because, unlike in most other Western cultures where it is uncommon for three generations to live in the same house, it is much more of a cultural norm to find this situation among Italians, with more often than not a grandparent living with their son, daughter or grandchild.

This extended family, still seen in many Asian cultures too, can bring its stresses and strains, of course, and it has fallen out of favour in many Western countries – parents can feel cramped and judged by having their folks there 24/7 as they attempt to bring up their children their way.

The momentum for this dissolving of the extended family hasn't just come from new parents, though; change has also been driven by a new breed of grandparents who enjoy both health and wealth and who quite frankly have other things to be doing with their time and money. They've done all the hard yards parenting-wise and they are going to enjoy their retirement together.

That is not conducive to covering school pick-ups and drop-offs three days a week.

But why should it be? Why should grandparents swap a golden period of their lives – one that they have almost certainly dreamed about while grafting for all those years – for more of the same?

Could it be that this generation of parents imagined they would get the support from their own folks that had perhaps been given by their great-grandparents and that they themselves remember fondly as children?

Robert Atchley, PhD, co-author of *Social Forces and Aging: An Introduction to Social Gerontology*, thinks so, but goes on to suggest that the grandparental involvement we may have received could well have been foisted upon our nanas and granddads purely because that is precisely what was expected of them. 'What you're really talking about is cultural images of what grandparents "ought" to do,' says Dr Atchley.

It's certainly true that in the United States today most parents turn to day care or nannies for routine childcare. Where grandparents do assume care for children it's typically only after a crisis in the family. Of the 7.7 million children in the US currently living with a grandparent, 3 million rely on their grandparents for most of their basic needs, with many living below the poverty line.

It's a very different story in China, where, according to the Shanghai Municipal Population and Family Planning Commission, a whopping 90% of the city's young children are being looked after by at least one grandparent – and half of these grandparents provide exclusive care, a number that's apparently on the rise.

It's a similar picture in other cities across the booming country too, with 70% of children in Beijing being cared for by a grandparent and around half of all children in Guangzhou.

So why is it that Chinese grandparents are much more willing to mind the baby? China's early retirement age – 60 for men and sometimes even younger for women – together with the one-child policy will undoubtedly have had an effect. Beyond the practicalities, though, another big factor, despite the enormous change China has seen over the past 20 years, is the pull of traditional culture. The long history of grandparents not only living with their extended families but also participating in child-rearing has, so far at least, proved to be more resilient in China than in the West.

In Britain, however, a nation further down the track when it comes to urbanisation and its demands, there seems to be a split.

For the many millions of people who long since moved away from their parents to hunt for work, asking grandparents to help (whether they want to or not) just isn't an option. But many of those who still live close enough to do so are leaning on their parents in numbers not seen for decades – the increase in the number of families with young children where both parents work is the obvious driving force.

This hidden army of go-to grandparents is increasingly helping out British families who are finding themselves priced out of the childcare market. According to charity Grandparents Plus, almost 2 million grandparents have cut their own working hours to help their children make things work at home. With childcare costs reported to have risen by 27% in the past five years, as well as putting in the childcare hours, the bank of nana and granddad is also being called upon more and more, making an estimated contribution of as much as £8 billion each year in the UK alone to ease the burden on hard-up and under-pressure parents.

While research shows that 3% of grandparents currently contribute financially, 13% expect to have to help children and grandchildren pay for their university fees in the near future. When asked, the majority said that they would dip into savings or use investments or property wealth to make that happen.

So it seems that in many parts of the globe, grandparents are once again vital to the parenting process – and that ancient history might just be repeating itself.

Teenagers
Can anyone else work them out, or get them out?

I 've noticed that being the first in a group of friends to have children results in the occurrence of a pioneering parental phenomenon.

Generally, the couple who took the plunge earliest in life acts, unwittingly, as a Trojan horse for the rest of the circle of friends – and that was certainly the case where my little crowd was concerned.

The rest of us watched in abject fear, laced with a healthy helping of wonder, as they negotiated the brutal first year – 'But when do they actually get to sleep or eat?' we whispered to each other.

Through weaning, biting, potty training, first days at school and tooth fairy visits, the lead couple have tested the water and have taken the big blows for the rest of us – they have carved a path for us to follow that, while not exactly smooth, is certainly more defined than the wilderness they had to cut their way through.

Now, though, these brave leaders are telling the rest of us that the parental phase they have recently entered makes all that preceded it look, well, like child's play.

The teenagers have landed.

These beings with their languid limbs, baleful looks and use of sounds rather than actual words to communicate are an altogether different proposition, our first-up friends tell us.

Is it like this everywhere, though? And was it always the case that being aged between 13 and 19 meant that you felt, acted and were seen to be so different?

The teenage timeline

History is littered with often brutal rites of passage rituals that have marked the transition from childhood to adulthood – especially, it seems, for boys.

From young Aboriginal boys being sent on a six-month solo walkabout in the harsh Australian outback, to the young Maasai of Kenya being given the small task of killing a lion with nothing more than a sharp stick and their sheer nerve, becoming a man was not for the faint-hearted.

(By some considerable distance the most bizarre, gruesome and cruel ceremony of all is the Sambian purification of Papua New Guinea – look it up at your peril.)

Despite these transitional ceremonies, though, there's a strong case for the origin of the distinct period of teenagerdom to be found in 1920s America. Against the backdrop of the First World War (not to mention the Spanish flu pandemic, which killed 3% to 5% of the world's population), something changed and American adolescents began displaying traits hitherto unknown among children and adults.

Although the word 'teenager' itself did not come into use until decades later, the teenage mindset really did begin in the 1920s, and with so much death and destruction in their recent past to remind them of the fragility of existence, living for the moment, breaking the rules and enjoying life began to be the watchword of the teen.

But it took a very practical invention to allow this revolution to take place, to give it legs. Or rather wheels.

The new-fangled but, thanks to Mr Ford, increasingly prevalent car gave American teens a freedom from parental supervision unknown to any previous generation in history.

The courtship process in particular was rapidly transformed. Up until this point, courting boys and girls had no choice but to spend their first dates at home, with such exciting items on the agenda as sitting in the parlour and dinner with the entire family. Then, after several visits, an unchaperoned walk to church or town might be sanctioned.

The car crashed through those homely conventions in an instant. Dating was born and was removed at once from the careful gaze of parents. Not only did the privacy afforded by the car usher in a sexual revolution in the US, it also meant that excited young things were able to look beyond their own towns and transport themselves to whole new dating grounds.

The petrol engine also played another part in helping to create teenage culture, by facilitating the birth of the high school. Once buses could transport students further from their homes, the one-room local schoolhouse was dead. What took its place saw larger numbers of teenagers than ever before being brought together daily – and a culture was soon born that has, in the century since, been exported around the globe.

But as well as the historical, cultural and social contexts around the world, in recent years there have been some serious physiological discoveries that suggest that the teen years really are different and that for a while we genuinely are in a period of our lives like no other.

Take sleep.

The big sleep

Teenagers are capable of generating shut-eye in quite staggering amounts. You remember the lie-ins from your own youth, of course, but when you encounter them again first hand, the sheer quantities involved take your breath away.

Laziness? Rebelliousness? Thisduvetistooniceness?

All three occasionally, no doubt, but there is also something much more physiological going on. New research from the University of Dundee[100] has shown that changes brought on by puberty result in a big shift in biorhythms, meaning that adolescents get tired later at night.

Throw in the tendency to study late and to use devices right up to and including bedtime and your average teenager won't fall asleep much before 11p.m. Then factor in that they are growing like topsy and something in the region of 8½ to 9½ hours of sleep are needed to function properly. A situation that has led to the influential American Academy of Pediatrics (AAP) to call for later school start times to reduce chronic sleep deprivation among teens.

The AAP says the issue is very much a public health concern and that lack of sleep in the young is linked to obesity, depression and the high prevalence of youth car accidents. Not only that, they say, but teenagers' school grades will also improve, as concentration skills and the ability to problem solve and retain information all get better with more shut-eye too.

So letting sleeping teenagers lie seems to make a lot of sense.

Taking risks and talking back

What about heightened risk taking? Or bolshiness, as it was known in our house.

Isn't that just a modern, Western phenomenon that sees teens with too much time and money on their hands acting like brats?

Not according to Laurence Steinberg from Philadelphia's Temple University,[101] who says that it's not only universal across all human cultures, but can also be seen in all other mammals too.

It might well be risky to leave the safety and security of your parents, but it seems that there is a biologic basis for the behaviour. Because risk taking is good for the gene pool it is rewarded and seems to be hardwired into teens, and therefore it comes out more and more as they approach the age when they take the biggest risk of all and step out on their own.

In the brain, what drives this behavioural change is competition between different brain systems, the socio-emotional and cognitive control networks. Both are maturing during adolescence, but at different rates. The socio-emotional system, as you may have guessed, takes care of social and emotional information and can become very active during puberty, leading to intense emotion, mood swings and sensitivity to social influence and peer pressure – a lot of which characterises the way teens are viewed in many cultures.

The cognitive control system, however, is the brain area that regulates our behaviour and makes the ultimate calls on what we do and when we do it. This particular chunk of grey matter doesn't finish maturing until at least our mid-twenties – so you've got an overactive social and emotional centre relying on a still maturing decision-making core to make the right calls.

Is it any wonder things go a bit pear-shaped every now and then with that combination on the go?

Whatever language it's delivered in, it also seems that the giving of backchat to parents is another important development stage rather than just a sign that today's teenagers are a disrespectful bunch. Their argumentativeness is, odd as it may seem at the time, the way teenagers build up the ability to have the strength to reject peer pressure from outside the home. By taking you on and arguing about absolutely everything under the sun, they are developing the fortitude to stand up to others and, crucially, to become their own person. The more secure a bond between teens and their parents, the more they will push the boundaries and be able to be fine upstanding individuals, strong of character and true of deed.

Which is something to cling to, when you're having the umpteenth argument that day with your 15-year-old about tattoos or the TV remote.

So if some of the mysteries of why teenagers behave the way they do are beginning to be explained by science, in time the cross-cultural labelling and stereotyping of them will be rewritten too. But there's still a long way to go.

For instance, ask most adults on the streets of London, Paris or New York if today's young teens are trying drugs or alcohol in greater numbers than ever before and the answer more often than not will be a resounding yes. But much like crime and population figures, the common misconception of negativity or threat is often far from true when the facts are consulted.

Figures show that both the number of 11- to 15-year-olds who took drugs in the UK in 2013 and the number who tried alcohol fell consistently – and have been falling for a decade.[102] It's a similar story in the USA too.

A number of factors are thought to be behind the trend, with one being that we are simply just getting better at parenting.

Go us.

Becoming better at caring for our children, and especially showing love and tenderness in the crucial first five years of life, is believed to significantly reduce levels of excessive drinking and drug taking later in life.

It's also proposed that today's teenagers are so busy with a cornucopia of extracurricular activities that there's barely a spare moment to experiment with anything between being picked up and dropped off by parents.

One such distracting factor in particular is likely to be playing a big part in this decline in drug and alcohol use among teenagers across Europe and the United States. What we are looking for is a global, cross-border phenomenon that has somehow moved our young away from substance misuse and towards something else, which may turn out to be equally addictive.

Step forward the internet, social media and gaming – the digital drugs!

While going to the park with a covertly purchased bottle of cheap cider might have felt the very height of cool and derring-do 20 odd years ago, the ability to explore virtual worlds with people from across the globe, or talk with someone your age on Twitter while their country goes through a historic revolution, seems, for some unknown reason, to be topping the appeal of the four-pack on the park bench or the surreptitious joint on the street corner for many of today's teens.

What's more, while this generation of teenagers is getting more and more connected, the previous generation or two made it their business to get disconnected – disconnected as a newt, in fact. Could we be about to enter a global age of role reversal for parents and teenagers? While the grown-ups keep up the vices they formed in their youth, is this generation of young adults, with their innate sense of worldwide connectivity, going to blossom into good global citizens from an earlier age than their old folks did?

The question of when does a teenager transition into an adult is a complex one, of course. Perhaps a good indicator of when a country classes its young people as being capable of thinking and acting for themselves is the age of sexual consent – and it's certainly a mixed picture.

In Europe, 16 is the most common benchmark, with countries including the UK, Cyprus, Finland, Georgia, Latvia, Lithuania, Luxembourg, the Netherlands, Norway and Switzerland all settling on that age.

In the Czech Republic, France, Denmark and Greece it's 15, while in Austria, Germany, Portugal and Italy it is 14.

Until recently, Spain had one of the lowest ages of consent in the world at just 13, but it has recently brought in legislation to raise this to 16.

Outside Europe there are even bigger variations. In Bahrain, for instance, the age limit is set at 21 and it's 18 in Iraq.

Some countries have different limits within their own territories – Australia's age of consent varies between 16 and 17 depending on where you are, and the same goes for America where it ranges from 16 to 18 from state to state.

At the other end of the spectrum, the likes of Brazil, Peru, Paraguay, Ecuador and Colombia all set it at 14 while in Japan, under certain circumstances, sex at 13 is even permissible.

Such a broad variation of ages shows that there is far from consensus on Planet Parent about when childhood ends and adulthood begins.

This schism is reinforced by the fact that, while there are 160 million children across the world's poorest nations whose situations dictate that they must work,[103] with over half of them doing so in hazardous conditions, there's a growing phenomenon in many of the world's richer nations that is seeing childhood being extended way, way beyond the teenage years.

The boomerang babies

In Italy they call them *bamboccioni*, or big babies.

In the UK, its KIPPERS, kids in their parents' pockets, and in the US they're simply known as the boomerang generation for their ability to keep on ending up back on the couch.

The adult child still living at home in their twenties, thirties and even forties was once unusual enough to be a comedy character staple. Now it's becoming so commonplace that for many it's no laughing matter.

A recent *New York Times* article gloomily entitled 'It's official, the boomerang kids won't leave' has caused an online tidal wave of parents to surge forth with tales of full bedrooms and empty fridges.

But it seems that this is a truly cross-cultural trend, and it is being driven by the long tail of the economic crisis that struck most of the developed world in 2007–8.

As young people from Baltimore to Brighton have failed to find jobs, economic independence and full-blown adulthood have become an unachievable pipe dream for many.

Traditionally, Europe's child–parent cohabitation rates have always tended to be higher than in the US, with Scandinavian nations and the Netherlands having slightly fewer young adults living with parents than, say, France or the UK, and southern and central Eastern Europe seeing the biggest number of stay-at-homers.

But the economic meltdown has seen territories across the board witness a sharp increase: figures show that 36% of 18- to 31-year-olds now live with their parents in the US, while in the EU the average figure is a truly astonishing 48.3%.

It's Italy where this issue has really become a national obsession, though. When a judge ruled that a 60-year-old Italian father still had to pay an allowance for his 32-year-old daughter because she was still living under his roof without a job, it prompted one government minister to propose a law making it mandatory for children to fly the nest at 18. Italy tops the tables not just by having an average age of home leavers at 26 years of age, but also because, even when they do move out, they live a shorter distance away from their parents than children in anywhere else in Europe – a mere 15 miles, on average, which by anyone's standards is close enough to take your washing back to *mamma*.

But perhaps we're looking at this the wrong way. Perhaps we should welcome this trend as the beginning of a backlash against the hitherto relentless flow of individualism that modernisation has brought with it.

Perhaps the breakdown of the centuries-old extended family, which urbanisation and industrialisation undoubtedly brought about, is beginning to be reversed. Perhaps the sustained economic hardship of the past decade has brought us back together because, ultimately, we need each other and are better off together.

Perhaps it's about time the boomerang did come back.

Either that or we need to change the locks.

A parent's perspective

于彩丽/Shirley – China

Like most of my female friends I am now living with my husband's mother in Beijing. Although my parents live very far away they do come to help us too.

I count myself very lucky to have them to help, which leaves me with enough time and space to concentrate on my work. I feel very grateful to my mothers, especially my mother-in-law – besides looking after the baby, she helps to do the housework and makes every meal for us. Importantly, I guess my daughter will learn how to be hard working, highly efficient and tidy from her too!

Obviously, the relationship between the mother-in-law and the wife can be difficult, but if there are ever any problems I compromise because all I have to do is think about what she does for us and whatever the issue was disappears!

My husband is my daughter's favourite love! He spends most of his spare time on his little angel and is a very good father. I'm not jealous at all – the better their relations are, the happier I am. Nowadays if feels like half of fathers around me are good fathers.

As for my life as a modern mother, I have five days concentrating on work and two days enjoying my motherhood and I try my best to balance the two.

I don't necessarily agree with mothers looking after their baby themselves for the entire time anyway. I have a friend who does believe that and the more time she spends on the baby, the harder it is becoming for her to leave to eventually go to work. She will end up thinking that she is the only one who can take care of her baby well in this world.

WORLDLY WISDOM - THE FINISHING TOUCHES

In the US, mothers are now the sole or primary income provider in a record 40% of households with children – that's nearly four times the rate in 1960.

Some 70% of Japanese women still give up work as soon as they have their first child. Japanese men are then also far behind their counterparts elsewhere when it comes to helping out around the home and with childcare; studies have shown that Japan's fathers spend on average just 15 minutes a day with their children.

As people lived longer, the evolution of grandparents thousands of years ago – and the extra help they could give with raising children – is thought to have been a key factor in helping us rule the planet! Having nana and granddad around to help is that important!

The concept of the teenager as we know it today is thought to have been created in 1920s America.

The newly invented car was a big catalyst in the teenage revolution, affording privacy, mobility and freedom from parental supervision, something that was unknown to any previous generation in history.

A teenager's brain is definitely wired differently. Research has shown that their overactive social and emotional centre, coupled with a still maturing decision-making core, has a lot to answer for.

The economic meltdown has seen territories across the world witness a sharp increase in grown-up children staying at home. In the US, 36% of 18- to 31-year-olds now live with their parents, while in the EU the average figure is a truly astonishing 48.3%.

Journey's end
So is there a parenting paradise?

We've made it from fertility to the final knockings of childhood and have unearthed plenty of cross-cultural nuggets along the way, but have we discovered a parenting paradise, a blissful utopia where nurturing your young is a sure-footed, guilt-free breeze?

Have we identified on our travels a nation that can categorically be described as the best place on earth to bring up your children?

Of course not. The adage that as a parent you are only ever as happy as your unhappiest child holds true from Nairobi to Newcastle, Beijing to Brasilia. No one has fully cracked it, or found the perfect parental formula, because it simply doesn't exist.

What is beyond doubt, though, is that rather than viewing each other's techniques and tricks as curious at best and downright odd at worst, in many parts of Planet Parent we really have begun to ditch the blinkers, put national traits and even parental pride to one side and really take on board what we can learn from each other when it comes to raising our kids.

Britain, for instance, has at long last started to implement some of the long-held fundamentals of how French children eat at school – from banning vending machines and junk food to making water the drink of choice at mealtimes.

Then there's the extraordinary story of kangaroo care, the instinct to hold your baby to your chest that had been lost in medicine among the incubators and complicated kit until adversity and sheer desperation forced one Columbian doctor to rediscover it and revolutionise premature baby care in the process.

The world of education is practically awash with global idea trading too, with Finland in particular continuing to play host to delegation after delegation as other countries and cultures attempt to find and replicate what is seen as their magic classroom formula.

In fact, as we've seen, if there's one region that seems to top league tables again and again when it comes to bringing up their young, it's Scandinavia. If you were to nudge Denmark and the Netherlands in that direction too, to create a Scandi Nordic Orange Great Dane of a geographical block, you really would have a slice of Planet Parent that seems to be consistently excelling in a wide range of parental areas – right from labouring mothers and childcare provision to education systems and childhood health.

But does that constitute evidence that the child-rearing code is finally being fully cracked in that part of the world?

Nope.

They have their problems like the rest of us, of course. In fact, recently in Sweden a fierce debate has begun, questioning the consequences of the very child-centric approach at which the rest of the world has often looked on in envy.

At the centre of the discussion is David Eberhard, a Swedish psychiatrist and father of six who published a book called *How Children Took Power*. He suggests that oversensitivity to children and a reluctance to discipline them has bred a nation of *'ouppfostrade'* or 'badly raised children'.

Nothing is straightforward in the land of the parent!

What's more, there's no doubting that globally we face some incredibly serious parental challenges in the near future, with the scourge of childhood obesity at the very forefront of those.

Perhaps less immediately obvious is the impact the incredible march of technology will have on our children as their touchscreen habit becomes more and more entrenched and all encompassing.

And it isn't just them who are seeing their behaviours changed by the smartphone and the tablet.

As part of its State of the Kid survey, US magazine *Highlight* asked 1,521 children aged between six and 12 if they felt brushed aside and ignored by their parents – a worrying 62% of them said yes.

And the main culprit cited as causing this mass parental distraction? The mobile phone, of course.

And when the same panel of youngsters were asked to name the best time to attempt to get some actual (as opposed to virtual) face time with their parents to talk about something important, 33% said mealtimes, followed by 29% opting for bedtime – because they were both blessed phone-free zones.

But, as we've seen, just as we can develop our own parenting skills by looking at how things are done elsewhere in areas as diverse as potty training and breastfeeding, discipline and learning, so the answer to these new problems will surely come from within our number.

Despite the differences and distances between us, Planet Parent is getting smaller. And the fact that we are all attempting the same difficult yet glorious job means that we have much more in common with each other and therefore more to learn from one another than ever before.

References

1. www.bbc.co.uk/news/magazine–24835822

2. www.bbc.co.uk/news/magazine–24835822

3. www.nature.com/nature/journal/v412/n6846/full/412543a0.html

4. Zita West, *Guide to Fertility and Assisted Conception*, London: Vermilion, 2010, pp135–50.

5. www.nytimes.com/2007/03/14/health/14iht-snvital.4906063.html?_r=0

6. www.smellandtaste.org

7. www.vanguardngr.com/2013/05/can-eating-yams-really-give-you-twins/

8. www.sciencedaily.com/releases/2012/12/121218203517.htm

9. economix.blogs.nytimes.com/2013/07/01/americas-new-mothers-among-the-youngest/?_php=true&_type=blogs&_r=0

10. www.eshre.eu/Guidelines-and-Legal/ART-fact-sheet.aspx

11. metro.co.uk/2013/02/05/robert-winston-a-lot-of-couples-are-exploited-by-the-colossal-fees-certain-ivf-clinics-charge–3380910/

12. www.medscape.com/viewarticle/723224

13. www.webmd.com/baby/features/7-tips-getting-pregnant-faster?page=2

14. www.bmj.com/content/336/7643/545

15. www.fertility.org.uk/news/pressrelease/10_03-Acupuncture.html

16. www.fertstert.org/article/S0015–0282(11)02859–7/abstract

17. summaries.cochrane.org/CD006920/acupuncture-and-assisted-conception

18. www.psychiatry.emory.edu/PROGRAMS/GADrug/Feature%20
Articles/Mothers/The%20effects%20of%20maternal%20stress%20
and%20anxiety%20during%20pregnancy%20(mot07).pdf

19. www.kybeleworldwide.org/041013-the-pain-of-childbirth---
differing-cultural-perceptions.html

20. www.heraldsun.com.au/news/just-put-up-with-pain-of-
childbirth-uk-professor-dr-denis-walsh/story-e6frf7jo–1225749426190

21. A. Chan, J. Scott, A. M. Nguyen and L. Sage, *Pregnancy Outcome
in South Australia 2005*, 2006, Adelaide: Pregnancy Outcome Unit,
South Australian Department of Health; www.birthbythenumbers.
org/?qa_faqs=epidural; S. Alran, O. Sibony, J. F. Oury, D. Luton and
P. Blot, 'Differences in management and results in term delivery in nine
European referral hospitals: descriptive study', *European Journal of
Obstetrics, Gynaecology and Reproductive Biology*, 2002, 103(1): 4–13.

22. www.asahq.org

23. www.mcgill.ca/files/ihsp/WFEIFinal2007.pdf

24. www.ilo.org/public/english/standards/relm/ilc/ilc87/rep-v-1.htm

25. www.savethechildren.ca/document.doc?id=305

26. news.bbc.co.uk/1/hi/health/1642676.stm

27. www.bellydanceforbirth.com/flex/a_conversation_with_three_
midwives/67/1

28. www1.hollins.edu/faculty/saloweyca/Athenian%20Woman/degra/
website.htm

29. unusualhistoricals.blogspot.co.uk/2012/11/medicine-medieval-
childbirth.html

30. englishhistoryauthors.blogspot.co.uk/2012/01/gossip-in-early-
modern-england.html

31. www.savethechildren.org/site/c.8rKLIXMGIpI4E/b.8682793/k.
EAB5/State_of_the_Worlds_Mothers_2013_Infographic.htm

32. ngm.nationalgeographic.com/print/2006/07/bipedal-body/ackerman-text

33. www.who.int/mediacentre/factsheets/fs348/en/

34. www.theguardian.com/news/datablog/2010/apr/12/maternal-mortality-rates-millennium-development-goals

35. muse.jhu.edu/journals/bulletin_of_the_history_of_medicine/summary/v070/70.3er_wilson.html

36. ajcn.nutrition.org/content/72/1/241s.full

37. www.bbc.co.uk/news/health–27373543

38. Tina Cassidy, *Birth: A History*, London: Chatto & Windus, 2007.

39. www.bbc.co.uk/news/health–22888411

40. www.oecd-ilibrary.org/sites/health_glance–2011-en/04/09/index.html?itemId=/content/chapter/health_glance–2011–37-en

41. www.slideshare.net/mobile/lizsmulian/infant-and-maternal-mortality-in-the-tibetan-community

42. www.savethechildren.org.uk/sites/default/files/images/State_of_World_Mothers_2013.pdf

43. blogs.lt.vt.edu/maxsoxrex/stereotypes-that-teachers-have-judging-students-by-their-names/

44. www.welt.de/vermischtes/article4550763/Achtung-diese-Vornamen-schaden-Ihrem-Kind.html

45. www.bounty.com/news-flash/teachers-pets-and-pests

46. science.nichd.nih.gov/confluence/display/cfr/Mothers+and+Infants+around+the+World%3A+A+Report+of+the+Cross-Cultural+Data+Collection+at+Five+Months

47. www.sgiquarterly.org/feature2009Jan–2.html

48. www.sgiquarterly.org/feature2009Jan–2.html

49. www.history.vt.edu/Ekirch/sleepcommentary.html

50. faculty.washington.edu/chudler/worldsl.html

51. www.oecd.org/unitedstates/
societyataglancerevealsevolvingsocialtrendsinoecdcountries.htm

52. www.medpagetoday.com/MeetingCoverage/APSS/9814

53. www.cbsnews.com/news/chronic-sleep-deprivation-linked-to-childhood-obesity/

54. www.ox.ac.uk/news/2012–01–11-crying-out-loud-baby-cries-get-speedy-response

55. news.nationalgeographic.com/news/2009/11/091105-babies-cry-accents.html

56. www.telegraph.co.uk/health/children_shealth/9286683/Babies-left-to-cry-feel-stressed-research-finds.html

57. www.nytimes.com/2005/10/09/nyregion/09diapers.
html?pagewanted=all&_r=2&

58. www.theguardian.com/lifeandstyle/2012/jul/06/change-your-life-neat-freaks

59. jpepsy.oxfordjournals.org/content/9/4/457.short

60. pediatrics.aappublications.org/content/109/3/e48.full

61. www.ncbi.nlm.nih.gov/pubmed/12175408

62. www.cnbc.com/id/50019795

63. www.ncbi.nlm.nih.gov/pmc/articles/PMC1988596/

64. www.ncbi.nlm.nih.gov/pmc/articles/PMC2684040/

65. www.ncbi.nlm.nih.gov/pmc/articles/PMC1988596/

66. www.dailymail.co.uk/femail/article–480407/The-return-wet-nurse.
html

67. Wright, D. (2007). Progress review: Maternal, infant, and child health. Retrieved June 6, 2008, from www.healthypeople.gov/data/2010prog/focus16/

68. www.oecd-ilibrary.org/docserver/download/8112131ec018.pdf?expires=1403001867&id=id&accname=guest&checksum=ACE78C116800 3FF3C946B2A1E22562DF

69. A. Maier, C. Chabanet, B. Schaal, P. Leathwood and S. Issanchou, 'Food-related sensory experience from birth through weaning: contrasted patterns in two nearby European regions', *Appetite* 49(2), 2007, 429–40.

70. www.telegraph.co.uk/news/3152142/Encouraging-children-to-finish-their-meals-could-fuel-obesity-crisis.html

71. www.theguardian.com/education/2010/mar/29/jamie-oliver-school-dinners-meals

72. www.odi.org.uk/future-diets

73. Food and Agriculture Organization of the United Nations, 2013, *The State of Food and Agriculture*, www.fao.org/docrep/018/i3300e/i3300e.pdf. Reproduced with permission.

74. apps.who.int/gb/ebwha/pdf_files/WHA67/A67_3-en.pdf

75. www.care2.com/causes/advertising-bans-work-quebec-has-lowest-childhood-obesity-rate.html

76. www.cerealfacts.org/media/Cereal_FACTS_Report_Summary_2012_7.12.pdf

77. Jean Aitchison, *The Articulate Mammal: An Introduction to Psycholinguistics*, Abingdon: Routledge, 1998

78. www.literacytrust.org.uk/assets/0000/1151/discussionpaper.pdf

79. www.dailymail.co.uk/sciencetech/article-2675577/Your-five-year-old-really-IS-better-working-gadgets-Researchers-toddlers-far-adept-learning-use-new-technology-parents.html

80. www.psychologicalscience.org/index.php/news/were-only-human/ink-on-paper-some-notes-on-note-taking.html

81. www.theaustralian.com.au/news/australian-children-in-danger-of-spending-more-time-in-front-of-screens-than-at-school/story-e6frg6n6–1226756092880?nk=a85a3c7841543914ae71fbe74b742f96§hash.GkwNA0oS.dpuf

82. www.aneki.com/watch_tv.html

83. www.commonsensemedia.org/research/zero-to-eight-childrens-media-use-in-america-2013

84. www.nytimes.com/2011/10/23/technology/at-waldorf-school-in-silicon-valley-technology-can-wait.html?pagewanted=1&_r=2&

85. www.nytimes.com/2014/09/11/fashion/steve-jobs-apple-was-a-low-tech-parent.html

86. www.parentingscience.com/effects-of-praise.html§hash.MgZLfZPW.dpuf

87. www.playthinklearn.org/Docs/Kim,+2009_JCB.pdf

88. www.unicef.is/efni/report_card/UNICEF_report_card_2.pdf

89. www.endcorporalpunishment.org/pages/progress/prohib_states.html

90. K. D. Bussmann, *The Effect of Banning Corporal Punishment in Europe: A Five-Nation Comparison*, 2009, Halle-Wittenberg: Martin-Luther-Universität.

91. onlinelibrary.wiley.com/doi/10.1111/j.1467-8624.2009.01341.x/abstract;jsessionid=464B7E786CAC667083A2E80D44BADD39.f02t01?deniedAccessCustomisedMessage=&userIsAuthenticated=false

onlinelibrary.wiley.com/doi/10.1111/cdep.12038/abstract?deniedAccessCustomisedMessage=&userIsAuthenticated=false

92. www.telegraph.co.uk/education/expateducation/8530207/Schools-in-Sweden-cant-be-beaten-corporal-punishment-around-the-world.html

93. www.worldbank.org/en/topic/poverty/overview

94. www.oecd.org/els/family/babiesandbosses-reconcilingworkandfam ilylifevol4canadafinlandswedenandtheunitedkingdom.htm

95. Based on data from OECD (2013), Employment rate of women, Employment and Labour Markets: Key Tables from OECD, No. 5, accessed on 5.12.14, http://dx.doi.org/10.1787/emp-fe-table-2013-1-en

96. www.familyandchildcaretrust.org/childcare-costs-surveys

97. docs.google.com/spreadsheets/d/tiZM_sgGPreQlZtOmjuXy4g/ htmlview?pli=1#

98. www.sciencemag.org/content/306/5702/1776.short

99. www.academia.edu/858223/American_Indian_Grand_Families_A_ Qualitative_Study_Conducted_with_Grandmothers_and_ Grandfathers_Who_Provide_Sole_Care_for_Their_Grandchildren

100. onlinelibrary.wiley.com/doi/10.1111/jsr.12096/abstract

101. cdp.sagepub.com/content/16/2/55.abstract

102. www.telegraph.co.uk/news/uknews/crime/10991641/Why-drugs-are-no-longer-cool-teenagers-are-internet-addicts-while-their-parents-snort-cocaine.html

103. www.ilo.org/global/topics/child-labour/lang—en/index.htm

Bibliography

Jean Aitchison, *The Articulate Mammal: An Introduction to Psycholinguistics*, Abingdon: Routledge, 1998

Adrienne Burgess, *Fatherhood Reclaimed, The Making of a Modern Father*, London: Vermilion, 1997

Tanith Carey, *Where Has My Little Girl Gone?*, Oxford: Lion Hudson, 2011

Tina Cassidy, *Birth: A History*, London: Chatto & Windus, 2007

Stacie Cockrell, Cathy O'Neill & Julia Stone, *Baby-proofing Your Marriage*, London: Collins, 2007

Dalton Conley, *Parentology*, New York: Simon & Schuster, 2014

Judy DeLoache & Alma Gottlieb, *A World of Babies*, Cambridge: Cambridge University Press, 2000

Judy Dunn, *From One Child to Two*, New York: Fawcett Columbine, 1995

Christina Hardyment, *Dream Babies*, London: Frances Lincoln Limited, 2007

John Holt, *How Children Learn*, London: Penguin Books, 1984

Deborah Jackson, *Three in a Bed*, London: Bloomsbury Publishing Ltd, 2003

David F. Lancy, *The Anthropology of Childhood*, Cambridge: Cambridge University Press, 2008

Brigid McConville, *On Becoming a Mother*, London: Oneworld Publication, 2014

Elizabeth Martyn. *Baby Shock!*, London: Vermilion, 2001

Planet Parent

Gill Rapley & Tracey Murkitt, *Baby-led Weaning*, London: Vermilion, 2008

Sue Palmer, *21st Century Boys*. London: Orion Books Ltd, 2008

Zita West, *Guide to Fertility and Assisted Conception*, London: Vermilion, 2010

Index